I Thought I Heard A Cardinal Sing
Ohio's Appalachian Voices

D1496165

photo by Sylvia Freeman

Edited by
Kari Gunter-Seymour

This publication was made possible by the Academy of American Poets with funds from the Andrew W. Mellon Foundation, with additional funding and support provided by the Foundation for Appalachian Ohio and the Ohio Arts Council.

ISBN: 979-8-9855242-0-8
Library of Congress Control Number: 2022930155

Editor: Kari Gunter-Seymour
Line Editor: Kristine Williams
Preliminary Jurors: Hayley Mitchell Haugen, David B. Prather
Cover Design: Kari Gunter-Seymour
Cover Art: Keith Wilde

Inquiries:
Kari Gunter-Seymour, Ohio Poet Laureate
www.karigunterseymourpoet.com
ohiopoetlaureate3@gmail.com

Published By:
Sheila-Na-Gig Editions
Russell, KY 41169
sheilanagigblog.com

I Thought I Heard A Cardinal Sing
Ohio's Appalachian Voices

Contents

In honor of our people and this rich Ohio soil

Introduction

I Thought I Heard A Cardinal Sing, Ohio's Appalachian Voices is a collection of poetry focused specifically on the unique cultural experiences of poets located in or connected to Ohio (Central) Appalachia. Within these pages you will find a lavish mix—Affrilachian, Indigenous, non-binary and LGBTQ; from teens to those creatively aging; poets in recovery, some differently-abled or with developmental differences; emerging and well established; some living in the state, others from assorted locations throughout the country—all with a deep connection to Appalachian Ohio.

People often forget and many do not even know that nearly 1/4 of the state of Ohio rests inside Appalachia proper, and pockets of Appalachian families who migrated generations ago prominently exist throughout the state, still firmly attached to their Appalachian roots.

The work speaks honestly and proudly as it represents Ohio's Appalachian population, providing examples of honor, endurance, courage, history, love of family, community, the land; and it provides evidence of how, even against the odds, our people continue to thrive and work hard to build awareness and overcome mainstream America's negative response to those with a strong Appalachian heritage.

The final pages of this publication do not include the usual standard contributor bios. Instead, I asked poets to prepare a brief written account, detailing their connection to Appalachian Ohio. The result is a compilation of statements that are as intriguing to read as the poetry itself.

Publication of this collection was made possible by the Academy of American Poets with funds from the Andrew W. Mellon Foundation. Additional funding and support was provided by the Foundation for Appalachian Ohio and the Ohio Arts Council.

My journey to bring about this one-of-a-kind collection has been a whirlwind of meticulously planned steps, to spontaneous decision making, gut laughter and head scratching. This service to my community is something deeply personal for me. A way of giving back, in honor of all who reached out to me, lifted me up and solidified my sense of pride in belonging to this extraordinary place.

Kari Gunter-Seymour
Ohio Poet Laureate, 2020-2024

Melissa Helton

The Elements

Migration to the colonies-turned-nation-
turned-empire: from farm to city,
suburbs to farm, cobblestone to asphalt,
city to mountains; sailboat, horseback,
train, carriage, steamboat, rural dirt
road, big wide highway;

continual dribbling south with each
generation: Massachusetts, New York,
Minnesota, Michigan, Ohio, Kentucky,
about to fall off into Tennessee; cross
river, fjord, ocean, canal, river, bog,
lake, channel, ocean, river, river.

What survived the Atlantic crossings:
knitting the German way, mint sauce
on mushy peas, the pragmatism
of the peasantry, malt vinegar on fish,
Pink Floyd, Protestantism, and how my DNA
rises up when I hear a hardanger fiddle
or bagpipes, some harmonic drone
to a sad melody, how mossy stones
know me, how fog shushes me still.

The rest is retroactive: Where
did momma's name come from? What
were the names on the vessels that
ferried them to this hemisphere? Who
gathered Hilda and the kids at Ellis
Island and ushered them west? Which
of my colonials brought disease,
drank whiskey while debating revolution? Why
did grandma's grandpa desert the New York
Cavalry during the Civil War? Who
survived the Nazi occupation of Norway? Does
the baby dad left in England know that

whatever man raised her isn't her blood? Why
did that ruined abbey in Wales
make me cry so hard?

Migration pushed few things
through the sieve, this push push
to be American: change your name,
change the food, the clothes,
the bending of your vowels,
which letters are still in the alphabet;
don't teach the children to speak
your own language; change until

we don't even know our names
nor where they've buried
our brothers nor to whom
they've married off our sisters.

Jonathan Graham

End of the Road

A road from long ago, of gray cinder and sandstone
crushed by iron-rimmed wheels

of wagons and heavy feet of oxen as they traveled Zane's Trace,
pulling all that was left from before

and promises for what would be, wandered through the weary coal town
of Midway. After crossing the shallows

of a wide Ohio creek, the road furrowed in mud as it climbed uphill
from the bottomland,

meandered past a strategic springhouse welcome to both livestock
and pioneer, then rested

at the Stone House Inn, brown and thick like an overcoat
on a blustery day.

There, in the afterimage of the moving light they followed,
a brimming trough of water

awaited travelers at the entry. Fresh water, shady cool and dripping
wet from lathered horses' mouths,

was as treasured in those early days of settling America
as it is today. They'd fill dry wooden barrels,

carry only enough on their Conestoga wagons to get them over
the horizon to the end of the road

where it fell from one world into the next.

Jonathan Graham

Painting the Mountain

In the kindest light
of morning,
we sat side by side
painting the mountain.
Just us two
on Christmas day,
facing the Appalachian
foothills, sunlight
above the steep cliffside
in our eyes.

Coal country
watercolorist by day,
classical violinist by night,
Mother, you made art easy,
natural, in-your-blood right.
When I tried to paint
the details of every
tree on the mountain
onto my canvas,
you leaned over
to tell me instead
to merge them,
be less exact,
allow the paint
to run free,
let the brush
tell me where to go.

Jonathan Graham

A Broken Song for the Willow Grove Mine Disaster

is nearly forgotten until a tremor shudders the ground.
            One clear morning
each March, a reminder at precisely the eleventh hour
            radiates from the 22 South tunnel,
a slight trembling
            by something from below
that disturbs a cardinal, momentarily off balance, his song
            of solitary notes
broken as he clutches a barren limb in a cold orchard
            of bending apple trees
on the hill above Willow Grove.

The comfort of a slight blanketing of snow, soft
            understanding in slanted rays of sun
of a world purely golden only at this given hour
            in winter light.
Shadows still of men in hard hats, colors encrypted in snow
            that blend with moving shadows,
one pastel, a young woman walking lively through the quiet
            to a parked vehicle
pauses for the tremor, feels something distant,
            unaware of the tunnel
and for seemingly no good reason but to look instinctively
            upward
through that ectoplasmic flash from a fleeting trance to stare
            briefly into the golden light.

She continues to strap her young son into his car seat
            almost identical
to her unmet uncle cinching the safety buckle
            on his miner's belt,
but before she starts the engine to go on, looks upward
            once more from the shadows to the sky,
pausing without ever knowing why. The cardinal,
            regaining his balance
on the limb, resumes his broken song.

Kari Gunter-Seymour

Because Coal

The last stars arc, dim the sash.
Wails the pitch of a coalmine's siren
quiver my temporal bone, a song to dig a hole.
My grandfathers, coal-caked, muscle
and blood, yoked to Peabody scrip,

sinking shaft or pit, railroad cars tippled,
cinder and soot smutting miles of track,
valley fills steeped in acid spoil,
one hundred years of forest sheared.

Pained as I am to reflect, my great-greats,
pigeon-toed, gap-mouthed, pondering
how the hard-working find themselves
both proud and begging, held fast,
like a flag that never waves.

Who hasn't rationalized themselves
a noble son or daughter, their life tightly
squeezed between two fists?

Tonight, roaming the ether,
I visit their graves, blush-pink peonies
to decorate each stone. Saying nothing,
I write, one finger in dust,
fire in our hearts, fire in our souls,
forever together, *down in the hole.*

Kari Gunter-Seymour

To No One in Particular

I am never happy to see summer go,
earth stripped of its finest voice.
I am sitting outside in my heavy coat,
porch light off. There is no moon,
no ambient distractions, the sky a Zion.

I take solace in considering the age
of this valley, the way water
left its mark on Appalachia,
long before Peabody sunk a shaft,
Chevron augured the shale or ODOT
dynamited roadways through steep rock.

I grew up in a house where canned
fruit cocktail was considered a treat.
My sister and I fought over who got
to eat the fake cherries, standouts in the can,
though tasting exactly like every other
tired piece of fruit floating in the heavy syrup.

But it was store-bought, like city folks
and we were too gullible to understand
the corruption in the concept, our mother's
home-canned harvests superior in every way.
I cringe when I think of how we shamed her.

So much here depends upon
a green corn stalk, a patched barn roof,
weather, the Lord, community.
We've rarely been offered a hand
that didn't destroy.

Inside the house the lightbulb comes on
when the refrigerator door is opened.
My husband rummages a snack,
plops beside me on the porch to wolf it down,

turns, plants a kiss, leans back in his chair,
says to no one in particular,
A person could spend a lifetime
under a sky such as this.

KB Ballentine

Something Sacred

The hollow of your neck is like the holler
I pass on the way to work –
a safe space for one who belongs.
A cove of shelter, kudzu tangling power lines,
lathering the hillside green,
even during the dark months. It's easy to hide
in that hollow when the world smolders
with heat and ash, where home's
bread and butter doesn't stifle
but sings, soothes. Mountains lean in,
checkered with wood-sorrel,
foamflowers, and ferns, dawn and dusk
just a variant of blue before night
folds in with scraps of stars. Shadows caressing,
coming close to whisper in that soft hollow.
To breathe in comfort, breathe away fear.

KB Ballentine

Blessing of the Birds

Day begins in mist — white and gray
   linen haunting the dawn.
I take tea to the porch, wait
   for cardinals to kiss
with beaks full of seed,
   for bluebirds to puff and ruffle feathers.

Steam from my cup a scrim
   for hummingbirds buzzing like motorboats.
It's been a grueling week,
   and the woodpecker hammers suet, hickory
like I've wanted to pound my fist.

Let the too-plain throat of the wren trill
   her silky notes until the haze burns blue,
cup empty — melodies and harmonies harvested,
     lifting,   lifting.

Dale Marie Prenatt

To the Part of my Spirit Still Up the Holler

To the part of my spirit
still up the holler near the
mountain break waterfall
past the gas line before the strip mine
where the horses got to play:

      I am not calling you back
yet. At extreme unction,
may I be so blessed
to recollect or recall at all, your name on my
lips will be my last act. In the dark

      slate of night you shiver through me
clear as a long horn blast warning
I sense us together
there — spread out over the whole
place breathing in the green world.

Jennifer Schomburg Kanke

Rock Riffle Road Homily

Sing now praises of chip and seal.
Five years to pass that levy. Joyful
Fords and Chevies as road dust doesn't
coat our cars, and ruts from spring rains
fill less deeply. Raise your voices,
glory to tiger lilies dotting
low spaces and ditches, Joe-Pye weed,
chicory, and teasel. But be not afraid to
dig some out when they've grown too dense,
stopping the flow of the runoff water.
They will begat anew come May Day.
Dance, dance, dance your abundance! July
brings the escape of the cow and her calf, though she
knows you are a respectful neighbor
calling her owner each year when she hides in
woods you pay the taxes on, enjoying
small moments of solace before her
young goes off to slaughter.

Jennifer Schomburg Kanke

They Came to Show How Safe the Mine
–After the Millfield Mine Disaster Nov. 5, 1930

Using sheets of burlap, mud and sticks
they built their nests like wrens,
whatever bits to block the gas.
Men were loading coal and thinking
on lunch when a wire hit the rail
back down an unused broken stretch.
What need was there for power on that line?
Small pockets of men scrabbled the shafts
to reach good air up near the top.
Rumor spreading fast as carbon monoxide,
top company men, cuckoos one and all,
were touring the mine that morning.
Some bodies were laid out in the pool hall,
others in the company store. A few burned
from the fire, eighty bloated and turned
as they tried to make their bodies use the unusable.

John Burroughs

My Me Mine

I'm going inside
hoping to be a lantern
not a canary.

John Burroughs

Come Pass

East and west
collide and mesh
in ways no mechanical
device can measure.

There is no true
north or south here
only our spiraling toward
what is and seems
meant to be.

Heart needles spin
like clock hands
but swifter and
less certain.

I take my direction from you.

Laura Grace Weldon

First Cool Day of September

Creekside lush with purple ironweed,
fluff-wrapped cattails,
Queen Anne's lace fairy skirts.
Please don't sigh when I pick another
bushel of warm red tomatoes, seeing
only the work ahead to preserve them.
Please don't bring up political storms
when trees brim with birdsong
and vines hang heavy with grapes.
Come with me to wonder
at this spiderweb, that fungus.
Let yourself feel the fizz
of gratitude. This is the lintel
across a door marked Peace.

Laura Grace Weldon

Common Ground

What's incomplete in me seeks refuge
in blackberry bramble and beech trees,
where creatures live without dogma
and water moves in patterns
more ancient than philosophy.
I stand still, child eavesdropping on her elders.
I don't speak the language
but my body translates best it can,
wakening skin and gut, summoning
the long kinship we share with everything.

Cathryn Essinger

Walking Away
–for Vivian

I don't stop to remove
the pebble from my shoe,

because it reminds me of home—

one step to remember,
another to forget.

William Scott Hanna

Cardinal

I know my mother's weeping is real by the way
she exhales, fragmented and flailing,

like someone newly mourning. My head only hip-high,
I stare up to her saddened face, too young to understand

any of this, but old enough to know something
is broken, and that with breaking, anguish follows,

old enough to know she would want to watch
the male cardinal she feeds every morning

newly perched in the bare Maple outside
the kitchen window. I nearly tell her to look,

to witness its bright red flame up against all
that white winter. But I wait, keep quiet

and listen, trying to hear in place of her grief,
the cardinal's song just beyond the glass.

L. Renée

2 Legit
–For visitation day with Dad, Summer, 1991, Columbus, Ohio

I was six then, but you had already taught me something about quitting:
      Quitting is for suckers. You said it like you had a green apple
Blow Pop souring the soft tunnels of your cheeks, caving them in like
      your lips were readying a plump pucker to plant on my temple,
which by then ached, my brow worried about what you worshiped,
      the cardboard pack of Kools in your left hand, held like a lover
or a daughter you once loved, your right hand lifting the skinny white stick
      to your mouth like I did peppermints at Christmas, waiting
on the stinging burn that felt like relief, absolution for my tongue,
      which, by then, had already been salt-slicked by slices of ham, string
beans & fatback, *too much of anything will kill you,* Mama told me, so I quit

      while I was ahead to live & make room for sweetness, her lemon bars
& brownies with walnuts & peanut butter crisscross cookies & cheesecake,
      topped always with sour cream & cherry pie filling, but it was not
Christmas, it was July, we were not waiting for your seasonal phone call,
      I was there with you, for once, in your car, *a hooptee,* you called it,
I had never heard that word, I was six, I knew only language with
      etymologies of conquerors, words like *cancer,* words embedded
with dying or leaving or deception, because thieves never have enough
      time to enjoy what they've stolen, since fear over somebody taking
what was never theirs is always there & so I learned about swollen veins
      that looked like crab legs creeping under the body's surface
in first grade, when Little Madeline said her Daddy was dying *cuz*
he can't stop puffin on white cancer sticks & how that Christmas
Mama had to tell me that peppermints weren't the babies of cigarettes,
      but the resemblance was enough to strike fear in my little girl heart,
like I had stolen time & it was coming back to collect me & collect
      you too, because of the resemblance, as if your prolonged absences
weren't their own kinds of death already, but what did I know, I was six

      when I saw your thumb press down a red lever like a PEZ dispenser
& there was no room for sweetness, just a single flame lighting the tip of mild
      menthol, the hiss of surrender like a bad spirit leaving the body after somebody's
Big Mama been up praying that sad hour don't nobody hear

but God & watched you suck in your cheeks like a fish on a hook
& watched you inhale that bad spirit before I had time enough to pray it away
& so I tried to conjure my best Clair Huxtable, practice the side eye
she never had to learn, The Look my Mama & every Black Mama I knew
knew like the back of their hands, their hands rarely needing to lift
from their laps to tiny butts, because The Look was enough to stop any Black
child with an ounce of home trainin as quickly as any threat of a switch,
which was never a threat, because by then you were already doomed & I didn't
want you to be already doomed & so I gave you The Look, its magic
freezing you mid-drag & I'll never forget the way your eyes widened, as if I had
sucker-punched you right in the nose & everything stopped & for a moment
you were a little boy heart & I was somebody else I knew but could not name
& fear entered then exited your eyes when you remembered,
like any good conqueror, that you still had the power & I felt the chill
of us resigned to our roles. *Girl, you looked just like my Mama*, you said,
then laughed at me.

Kip Knott

Sleeping in Grandpa's House, Hemlock, Ohio

I hear him wheezing in the next room
above the storm outside that blows reckless
as Duke the local drunk screeching home
from the Stonefront Tavern down Rte. 155
swerving from white line to yellow and back again
grief pulsing in his blood from heart to brain
with numbing speed like the Jack he drank
in the bar too dark to let him see
where cigarette smoke hung around his neck
like his guilty conscience
for when the checks stopped from Workers' Comp
and for the night his wife and son tried to provide
by going fishing on Buckeye Lake
in gale-force winds that scalloped waves
into obsidian blades sharp enough to gash the hull
and spill them into a water grave
where they tried to swim to shore
their chests tight as Grandpa's chest
when he used to set a charge in Peabody Mine #6
where he breathed the dark air that kept him alive
and drove the coal dust deep into his lungs

Kip Knott

What Two Bits Could Buy
–for Patsy Cline, 1932-1963

Your life ended not long after mine began.
I can't remember ever hearing you before
I turned twelve, twelve years after your death,
when your voice wept, dispossessed

from an outdated and battered jukebox
in the corner of a miners' dive bar in
Corning, Ohio, a carcass of a coal town torn in half
by the yellow gash of Sunday Creek.

It only cost two bits to release you
from the Wurlitzer coffin that some part of me
believed held some part of you
the way the altar of St. Bernard's held its holy relic.

My grandmother, the bartender every miner loved
to call "Babe," tossed me the special red quarter
she plucked from the back of the till.
I listened as the coin rattled down its metal shaft,

clicking and clinking like a round of shot glasses
struck on the bar after another cancerous shift.
It took a moment for the first high, lonesome violin
notes to wheeze between a cacophony of hacking

black lung coughs. But then, like a cry
rising above a crowd of smoke ghosts,
those permanent shadows each man dragged up
with him from an underworld without light,

your voice carried me off to a brighter place
where there were only "Sweet dreams of you."

Jean Mikhail

Bacon and Day

I won't be happy all the time.
I won't be happy even when you play
your banjo, your darling, even when
we watch *The Heehaw Variety Show*
on TV. I won't be sorry, no apologies
if I want to change the channel,
turn the dirty grooved TV dial,
with the filth of too many fingers touching.

We listen to Doc Watson play, blind
and he plays a banjo better than you ever will.
His hands cross over yours, instructing you.
It is a different style of playing, though—
more hillbilly, you say. More strings
attached to sorrow than you can play.

Your banjo is a Bacon and Day,
all Dixie. It actually chuckles at me, flashy
with its silver bridge to somewhere
happy with its bucked teeth grin of pearl
inlay, it plays the catchy tunes
like *The Happy Days Are Here Again*.
The taut white face smarts
from all the strum. You scratch
the hide with your fingers.
It purrs like a fat, white cat.

My mother's head and arms are in the oven,
in the kitchen, checking on the underside of ham
on its silver platter, where a tree is molded
on the tray's metal bottom. She picks it up,
and the hot red blood pools with juices
that fill the tree to overflowing,
and your hand keeps slapping,
your banjo laughing, rattling keys,
opening, opening, even though
you close and clamp down
because you are the saddest man I'll ever know.

Roy Bentley

Bright Lights and Country Music
–Bill Anderson

In nineteen sixty-five, I'm eleven and
listening to a Trans-Oceanic Zenith radio:
Bill Anderson is singing like country music
is God's voice. Nothing more, nothing less.

I'm a lanky kid lying in bed beside his father—
who is smoking a cigarette in a t-shirt and pajama
bottoms: a father who favors a music with twang
since we're hillbillies. They're on the mend, my

mother and him, having been divorced for some time.
Tonight, he's visiting from the town I will soon finish
growing up in. Grow old in. He wants me to say yes.
To the move. But he's talking dragging us to live

with strangers. We're listening to the Opry and he
says Gene Howard, his uncle, bought a floor-model
Zenith for the house he was raised in after his mother
was institutionalized. He describes them listening

on Saturday nights. 650 AM WSM out of Nashville.
After he says the word *sanitarium*, he turns off the light.
The dial of the Trans-Oceanic glows like a lit cigarette.
Like the one burning in his hand in shared darkness.

Roy Bentley

Beautiful Plenty

At 30, my father drove a Cadillac in all weather.
Maple seeds spun down onto the wax job of a hood,
a black hood, black his preferred color in automobiles.
He owned two Cadillacs. His and hers. Both of which
he forfeited divorcing my mother, who saw not a cent.
When the divorce was final, he remarried. Had a child
with another woman. Said that wasn't what he wanted,
another family. Some weekends, he came around. We'd
go on walks. I remember walking by the river in Dayton.
He said, *You know five rivers converge here* and named
four out of five by a botanical gardens gemmy with rain.
Then he said, *That's the Great Miami* and looked off in
the direction of an orchard, the bright and unforgettable
scent of the ripe fruit the definition of Beautiful Plenty.
On a bank, a rotted boat sat. Someone said every boat,
new or old, is looking for a place to sink. And he said
something similar, my father, no fan of boats. Maybe
he supposed the one we saw was like their marriage:
as gone to rot and about useless as the oars to row it.
My parents were poor kids from eastern Kentucky
who spoke a language of want I wasn't fluent in.
We never saw plenty again, thanks to him. It was
around that time my mother got a job in a factory.
Which must have pissed her off. Because she got
tough with the world and with herself. Tough and
satisfied because her face and Ava Gardner outline
glistened brighter than anyone with a beating heart
when she stood anywhere near that next car he kept
so immaculate you could see a version of yourself in
every shiny, midnight-black inch of fender and hood.
And when they got remarried, there was the matter
of the kid he'd had. Which she made him support,
though she wrote out the monthly checks herself
and stamped and mailed them. Just to be sure.

Susan Sheppard

The Indians on the Hill

Once my grandmother and her sister overheard a clerk in a small town
Dress shop whisper to the other: "Don't wait on them. They look like dagos."

Ashamed, the girls quickly left. They did not know what dago meant,
But they knew it must mean something bad.

Years later, high on a hill, earth gave way to buffeting winds, shook
The mulberry trees into fists. I dream-walked in skin slippers over rib cages

Of ancestors, inside the world's drum with faces broad as clay pots
As skeins of clouds layered back into the breath of woods.

Below me, in a tin-can house another Saponi grandmother sat
Under green awning, face dark as a chestnut, apron pinned to her dress,

Wearing men's shoes. The grandmother clutched her cane between her knees.
We stared. I crouched at the edge of her garden, I was five,

With umber wing of hair over my eye, face smeared with the war paint
Of pokeberries. She gazed through milky cataracts as

I grabbed dirt loose as soap powders then flung it
Where crows argued with the jays. Grandmother said nothing.

Lost in the purple cabbages, the glint of pie plates sent out codes
In the wasting sun, there was nothing for me to do but go home.

Later, red spirits multiplied into the evening, I felt them through my hair,
Glimpsed their spirits weaving through trees bloody and painted.

I see my Lenni-Lenape great-grandmother wringing cloth,
Rinsing pale moons of fingernails of sienna-skinned hands in creek water,

Only to be shut away later in the Trans-Allegheny Lunatic Asylum to die alone.
We never found her grave but fell into her way of drying out

Gourds for seed rattles hung like otter skulls from a rope.
Through the smell of dying fields, I ran into the arms of my grandfather

Who quieted the evening into dreams. That night we found crow feathers
Left on the stone walk like obsidian blades on the way to the toilet

And those eyeless pelts of fox stretched over the outhouse door.
Grandma stayed inside to stitch together

Cast off rags into wondrous designs. Grandma and her sister
Never went back to that store.

Susan Sheppard

Snap Apple Night

I fall asleep to the briar songs of witches,
Those who circle me with miniature bells
Attached to thorn fingers, the ones
That unflesh the golden fruit that falls
On some black, unholy ground,
Left to simmer and swarm
Like other brooding souls.
Among the bearded hags of trees,
I turn these stones into conjurer's bones
To let them to rattle in my pockets.
I know this darkness will cause
My cells to open like ghost flowers,
As my body hums alone on its bed
And my skeleton rises from its sleep
To walk down a lonely road.

Daniel Edward Moore

Less Than a Mile Away

A sabbath sunlight enunciates last week's wounds,
as goldens beams of Midwest prayers rise from the
world's monstrous book, a literary treasure of evildoers
with names that sound like neighbors ignored for fear of
what they'd say. Sunday is always happy to slow the
heart's little tractor down to a rusty, repentant, day of
regret when believers find comfort forgiving themselves
like wretched unplowed fields. If harvest is how the
Kingdom comes, shucking the world of the body's sin,
setting the unholy table of time with bent utensils of faith,
remember that's you in the wooden bowl covered in the
gravy of good and that's your neighbor's knees on the floor
less than a mile away.

Daniel Edward Moore

Fried Theology

Next to their house, in the hill's wounded side,
was a cold dark garage my Grandpa built.
In the far left corner between a shovel and hoe
stood three wooden poles crowned with sharp metal prongs,
death's summer gear for a hot August night, when we'd
wade down the creek blinding frogs with flashlights
before they could jump into their watery world
and escape being Sunday night's dinner.
Grandma would be on the porch with her knife,
a brilliant yellow halo adorning her head,
descending from the bug light above.
She had been reading her Bible for hours,
praying our sacks would be stained with the blood
of creatures we were given dominion over, according to Genesis 1.
She'd always hug me as the carving began,
hoping her affection made the carnage less brutal,
less likely to cause me any distress
as we started getting ready for church.

Elaine Fowler Palencia

My Beloved Dead Gather to Give Me Advice
in Good Hope Cemetery, Gallia County, Ohio

Chop your own wood
and carry your own water.

Agree with thine enemy
when thou art in the way with him.

Talk's cheap. Takes money to buy whiskey.

Tuck your thumb in your fist before you hit somebody
so you don't sprain it.

Don't have plastic flowers in the house.
Wear a slip so you don't show Christmas.

Work, for the night is coming.

Thou shalt not
Thou shalt not
Thou shalt not

Don't owe anybody but the bank
and don't owe the bank.

Plain words are easy understood.

You don't know a person
till you've wintered with them.

What goes under the Devil's belly
comes up over the Devil's back.

If you burn your rear
sit on the burn.

Get your lessons.
The more education you get
the lonelier you'll be
but it's worth it.

Don't sing any louder
than you can sing pretty.

Sufficient unto the day is the evil thereof.

You can't die on every man's cross.

Pipe down.
Straighten up.
Quit whining.

This too shall pass.

Respect your tools.

Keep your powder dry.

Steve Abbott

The Hills

Where, especially in autumn, something
is released, like spring pollen burning air,
to cling to the sleeve of a breeze carrying light
up a river valley on slim shoulders.
Like ancient burial grounds they rise,
rounded waves of russet and amber
telling stories of crossroads and back roads,
railroads and rivers, simplicity
sanctified in their comforting shadows.

Something shakes the trees
and a hundred or a thousand miles away
their children turn as one child
from desks and presses, from lullabies
and lovers, and from dreams and daydreams
they look up from wordless prayers
and smell apples.

In the next uneven breath
something snags and breaks, silently,
like an old woman's heart in a forgotten room,
and in that moment's collective release
a whisper stirs
a leaf of crimson and yellow
on a hill in southern Ohio.

Steve Abbott

Eddie on the Trestle, Scioto County, 1959

The coal train's pulsing approach and warning horn
a deafening fanfare to his late afternoon performance.
His body rippled with the landslide rumble,
his fingers wrapped around enough crosstie
to keep him vibrating to a sound too loud
for the boyish whoops to be heard as something like
an empty freight raced through his lungs and hung
his wide eyes high over a rock-dotted creek bed
thirty feet below, where rabbits shuddered
to the steady stampede of hoppers moving
northward over his head to wherever.

Long-shadowed light stretching his legs long
as the uprights, he danced with his squirming silhouette
to the shriek of steel on steel, closer than a heartbeat
to his face, power and mass passing within reach
and dripping adrenaline from each piece of
sky blinking between the cars.

In the fading beat of wheels, orange leaves were
brighter, yellows held light longer.
The way home swelled with new hues of shadow
and echoes no one else could hear
in a world all the more alive
for its laughing proximity to death.

Charles Salmons

Ode to Scioto Trail Swim Club
–For Roy Bentley

In South Columbus in the 1980s, American boys and girls
could have their pick of music to groove to, strutting
poolside during Late Night Swim at Scioto Trail Swim Club,
assuming their mothers and fathers could afford the price
of membership with blue-collar paychecks, Reaganomics
funding a war on drugs, and Republicans spewing
western rhetoric, pressing the Soviets to tear down the wall.

But what did middle and high school kids care about taxes
when there were skin and skimpy swimsuits to ogle
from the deep end, water polo street rules in the diving area.
We were mesmerized by how Old Man Blakeman's
daughter—already at sixteen—filled out a one-piece.
Music bounced through chlorinated air.
Sometimes we grumbled, sometimes we dug it.
Depends on the neighborhood we hailed from.
Our elders called for Cash, Kenny, or Loretta,
they too steeped in hill-country roots and rigor.
My brother and I argued Duran Duran versus Dokken.
Friends from L.A.—"Little Africa" our parents called it—
would thump Big Daddy Kane or Eric B. and Rakim.
Soon we got Run D.M.C. splashed with a little Steven Tyler
and Aerosmith, the formula for racial harmony set
before us on MTV.

> Except the right people weren't watching,
weren't listening, unwilling to consider their misconceptions.
But we were daring, took our digs and disagreements downhill
to the undersized basketball court with rigid rims that kicked
out long rebounds, frequent fast breaks, or to the ping-pong
table where a well-honed backspin meant you were the one
calling *Next!* long into evening. Cannonballs from the high dive
were never out of style, concession hot dogs never out of stock.
Only summer could burn out when Labor Day weekend signaled
a new school year. At the back of the bus, Walkmans pumped
"Brass Monkey," the hip-hop funk of inner-city Jewish boys
bursting beyond Brooklyn's boundaries into our ears,
those budding spaces where anything was possible.

Charles Salmons

On the South End, Too
–for Hanif Abdurraqib, after his poem
"All the White Boys on the Eastside Loved Larry Bird"

We loved him on the South End, too,
where our parents and grandparents identified
with hick-ness, they, too, born and raised
in the whites-only hills of Kentucky, West Virginia,
deep hollows where there were no fields
for football, baseball—just a utility pole
tall enough to nail a piece of plywood,
mount a hoop above a patch of gravel and dirt
alongside trailers our relatives still reside in.

We loved him because he loved the game.
We loved him because when Isaiah offered
the olive branch, he accepted it.

In my neighborhood, our elders would have broken
that branch across their knees, burned it,
used it as a switch across our backsides
for even thinking about inviting guys like you
into their homes. But we knew better,
knew the color of a man's skin meant nothing.
Only his game mattered.

It was the game that bonded us.
It was the game that taught us how to be men,
to say what you mean, mean what you say,

and be ready to back it up
when you lace up the high-tops, step
onto the asphalt, the concrete, shirts versus skins,
and take your opponent one-on-one
hard to the hoop on a July afternoon,
he and the sun double-teaming you,
their breath hot on your bare shoulders.

Shuly Xóchitl Cawood

Places I Looked for You
–after Natalie Kusz's "Now and Then I Look for You"

In every airport, at the last gate, in a plastic chair,
your head lowered, reading an article I might never understand,
or writing one, having the terminology for everything but *stay*

On side streets, especially in rain, pedaling a bike,
your yellow poncho flapping, like applause, like surprise,
like a bloom defying gray

In any soybean field, between rows of yesterday
and what might have been, standing in boots flecked
with hard day's dirt and the smear of regret

In every small city, in any blue truck
or back bedroom tinged with the day's last
drunken light that can soften and forget

At night, in dreams, never the same one, but always
we were young and we lay side by side like matchsticks
in a box, ready for the troubled flame

And I don't need to find you, not anymore,
but I know I will see you just once—in a crowd, on a train,
in a long line—and I wonder if I will know by then

the language for *I'm sorry,* for *goodbye*

Shuly Xóchitl Cawood

Some Kind of Prayer

What can I tell you that you do not already know?
Listen to the grass, its long legs whistling as it swishes.
Touch the brush of cattails, the brittle wings of pine cones,
the dry skin of chokeberries—feel
their burst. Taste rain. Say you're sorry

not for what you did but for how you doubted
yourself for so long. This life is filled
with a million cocoons and you can choose
how long, which one, or none.

Sleep is so close. Run now, run.

Jennifer Hambrick

Hands

her hands curve soft
as a wooden spoon,
the wrinkles at her wrists
are growth rings etched
into flesh like furrows
in the field beneath the hills
that watch the children
she bore the way the moon
bears light from a source
its beauty reflects. Before
the dawn of each new life
she climbed to the attic,
wet crescents under her eyes,
and wordless brought down
the chest of layettes
and tiny cloaks and trousers
she'd packed away
when the child she thought
would be her last outgrew them.
She was full of stories
she could not tell.
Light powders her sun-speckled
hands as she twists corn shucks
blonde and crackling
into ropes for the chair
where my grandfather
then my mother breathed
the words and silences
that made us, the lore
of reaping just enough
to see another day,
of the ones who died in birth
or war and the ones who
ran away, their lives left
lingering in the coils
of time. I am full of stories

I cannot tell, but my bones hum
like a harrow hitting rock,
melodies mingling in the half-light
of someone else's memories,
my hands twist the strands
of each day's tunes
into tomorrow's song,
these hands hold that song,
these hands let it go.

Jennifer Hambrick

Roots

they dig through all they have
to build that leaning house
on this dirt, to touch broken teeth

to meat or milk each day

a horse limps a rust-eaten plow
through a tangle of wasted stalks,
bridle clanging like a city facing west

where no one sees the dawn

the salt of their sweat in the furrows
rises on my tongue, stings
in the arches of my feet,

barbed wire nailed to rotting posts

pins me to a parceled tract
bought with barren work for those
who say their families never owned a slave

the horizon opens across the field

my legs work to steady on these ridges
gouged with the only tools on hand,
stretching through generations

still holding on to their wounds

Elizabeth Tussey

Columbiana County

Columbiana County cracks, issues fissures
through faults deeper than the shale veins

draped across river beds and sunken bones,
wakes trilobites, rankles the cantankerous dead,

breaks the solder of their iron caskets. I know
the hiss of ghosts slipping skyward, dragging souls

heavy with metals and Mirex fused to incorporeal shades
They weave a toxic sheen amid the air. I, too, am haunted,

my blood salted, unextractable even beyond the veil.
I bear my pall across state lines, across decades. I try

my tethers to an ailing home, recalled only through the fade
of fevered dreams and anchored to the anguish of my departed.

Elizabeth Tussey

Imperial Candlewick

My Candlewick crystal was once river silt, sulking
at the bottom of the Ohio, hiding with hellbenders
and box-springs and Big Gulp cups thrown
from Route 7 off the edge of Belmont County.

Spun delicacy separated from slag, in the same
hills that hold my kin in the anthracite embrace
of a mine collapse. I burn with furnace blaze
though the forge is snuffed and silent.

Now, the factory ruins beckon to the fentanyl-sick,
my river valley kin, separated only
by the difference in our inheritance of grace.

My candlewick crystal refracts the light, carries
the dormant heat of the forge, the incinerated past.

Michael Rainwater

Landscape W/ Figures

The leaves of the sugar maple are gone.
Light blue sky fades the curtains.
The woodstack, growing,
as father and son attend to the
remaining logs of elm.
Flash of axe and maul—
giving up on the cherry—
too green.

The short grass of the woodlot, brown
and patchy where the larger logs
have lain since mid June.
Wood chips and husky chunks of dried bark.
Stomp and clap of cracked leather boots.
Stink bugs, vast numbers of them,
spinning through the air like macabre dandelion fluff—
failing in the late cold and collecting in piles where they fall.

Further out, beyond the treeline and
twisting river's arm,
dust colored fields and feed corn still standing in odd rows.
Harvesters parked where their drivers got tired and went in for coffee.
No dawn or dusk now, just the rosy fading of the day.
Nights turning cold—
dark leaves collecting in the low places, where the sun runs out.

I have a hard time remembering
where the world ends and home begins.

Michael Rainwater

Going Home Again

That tractor over there—
turtle of the hill—
keeps rumbling rumbling.
Bring the fields in and hang them up to dry.
Long rows of deep huskbrown remembering.

    Five years removed,
    not every mum will know frost.

I passed down this road many times as a boy.
The one that winds by my mother's red house.
Testing the waters of one journey or another.
Always returning to the safe halo of the barn light
casting shadows and a warm analog glow upon the gravel driveway.

    Crickets in the tall grass
    around the water pump.

Years have passed now without me knowing—
my face is bristled, my head shaved.
Staring down a different road, this one paved and strange,
far from my mother's red house.
Another passing white line,
October drawing closer.
Following the north birds south, dusting
a winding line back to familiar fires.

I have many friends, but all at home and mostly in cities.
Alone on a ridge,
the floating world cackles.
Mountains sag into valleys.

    In the needles of a spruce,
    evening dew.

Christine Wilson

Rub and Conceal

Listen, a crisp, crinkling rustle like
the gathering of wadded notes with a broom
I shiver as the leaves rub and conceal
while I roll over the sound of the wind

The gathering of wadded notes with a broom
brings me to find a letter she wrote
while I roll over to the sound of the wind
these crumpled thoughts about betrayal's lies

bringing me to find a letter she wrote
Although uncovering only the second page
these crumpled thoughts about betrayal's lies
are whispering a story as old as their marriage

Although uncovering only the second page
I sense her holding on to his secret
whispering a story as old as their marriage
Written longing, yet her voice still echoes

I sense her holding on to his secret
stronger than either held to their vows
Written longing, yet her voice still echoes
Revealing one more time the restlessness

Stronger than either of their vows
and louder than the silence of a shared guilt
Revealing one more time the restlessness
An unnecessary death, an illicit way of life

Louder than the silence of a shared guilt
Listen, a crisp, crinkling rustle like
an unnecessary death, an illicit way of life
I shiver as the leaves rub and conceal.

Hayley Mitchell Haugen

The Blue Wife

read a story once about a woman
who walked into a cornfield, just left
her gaping husband at a roadside Super-Quick
and strolled into the embrace of night,
the fireflies closing the gaps behind her,
briefly lighting the spaces she had been.

Blue Wife, though, is no romantic: the forest
behind her house slowly encroaches,
all coyote howl and jaw bone, deer tick
and smothering kudzu. Poison ivy strangles
her shrubbery, darkens the sun porch walls,
and the hope that is the firefly, is too fleeting
to light the way.

Hayley Mitchell Haugen

Hannah amongst the Graves
–for Charles Kerns 8.9.1944 #931

Hannah is a picture amongst the graves,
her long hair whipping about in a wonder
of dark curls, spring rain unpredictable as madness.
She scans the rows of headstones, searching
for her great grandfather who retains his past,
his name, among the nameless dead of the asylum.

Two-thousand dead at the Athens Asylum
for the Insane, and their numbered graves
tip and slide into corrosion, sink into the past.
19, 84, 930: few remember, or visit, or wonder—
each number a page in the landscape's story, searching
for its reader, its interpreter of madness.

And what of madness?
Hannah seeks the secrets of the asylum:
intemperance could have set his loved ones searching
for assistance; or perhaps he was just mean and grave
or rakish, as her family has often wondered—
they were too young when he died to recall his past.

But from the dark eyes of the attic windows, the past
looms, spreading shadows that can drive one to madness.
How can she not think of him, how can she not wonder
about those days before Thorazine, the horrors of the asylum,
electric shock and lobotomies sending men to early graves
while the locals lunched on the hospital grounds, searching

for stones to skim across blue lakes. This search
for meaning haunts her family for generations past,
so they take up a collection, add his name to the grave,
but this, they know, is no cure for madness.
Does his ghost remain tethered to the asylum—
just one of many reported to roam in wonderment

at their own losses? Do they watch in silent wonder
at our modern advances? How Hannah finds herself, searching
for hereditary secrets etched in the records of the asylum:
For a glimpse of her future, she unearths her past,
whether she find love, or pain, or madness.
So hard to stifle that chill at these graves

as she wonders if the madness will strike her.
She searches the past: is there a warning in the DNA
engraved on the tomb of her heart—or asylum?

Diane Kendig

My Grandfather Leaving Pigeon

The first time, he went to Denver, where he also mined,
earned enough to return with a ring so thin it's now split,
still holding its diamond chip, given to my grandmother
when she was seventeen. They had all daughters,
which the uncles pitied him for, not one damned son.
But he adored the four, reveled in their small misdeeds
as darling, didn't scold except for his dark look
which could stop even Aunt Mad at her baddest.

So the second time, when he packed them all up
and moved to the city, living among the newest immigrants,
the Spaniards, Bulgarians, Romanians, and Hungarians,
I imagined it was for work. "Work?" shouted
Aunt Margaretta to me in her nineties, blind,
in a nursing home. "There was no work.
It was the Depression. He said
he wanted his daughters to get an education.
No one was going to get an education in Pigeon Run."

Pauletta Hansel

Pattern

My mother never followed a pattern
exactly as laid out
thin as snakeskin on the kitchen table.

It was the only time I ever saw her make a mess.
Days later, she would still be sweeping
straggled slivers of the dress

that my sister or I already wore.
Ours never looked exactly like the ones
beneath the label—Butterick, McCall.

She knew to bias cut the skirt
to skim our roundness,
add a row of stitches to the bust

we had yet to acquire.
I can't recall that either of us
ever thanked her

then. We wanted store bought, even though
she showed us how those flimsy things
came from the washer stretched and frayed.

Neither of us took her Singer
when she died.
My sister took some of the patterns

for the pictures, though the papers
never folded flat inside,
the way they'd come.

I still have the last dress she made me,
in my twenties, viscous rayon velvet
patterned from the one in Shillito's

she knew I never could afford.
I kept her sewing shears,
their broken blunted blades.

Pauletta Hansel

Adelaide, Hieronymus, Magdalena

I remembered granny's chaw, but not my grandpa's pipe
until I got a whiff from inside of some dead man's
Chrysler through the opened door, his people spilling out

onto the blacktop road I walk in any kind of weather,
ice or scissor weeds between its cracks.
The cemetery's filling up this spring, dirt piled

on graveyard grass, green that never dies back,
above forgotten bones with names nobody carries.
Walking here, I never thought of anybody's body

but my own, a little ache around the bends. That's how it is.
I'm older than my granny, then, out on the trailer porch,
her spit jar and her uncut rope of hair coiled tight,

mostly black the way mine's mostly not. Somebody
must have took my grandpa's pipe after he died,
the one I forgot. The door slams shut

and now they're all behind me on the road,
their cemetery flowers heaped on clods of clay.

Sherrell Wigal

Cardinal Singing

"Do not stand by my grave and weep
I am not there, I do not sleep"–Mary Elizabeth Frye

This morning at dawn my father came,
red-feathered, singing the cardinal song.
His death, one year gone, and I am anointed again
with his attendance pulling me into the day;
His celebrations slip silently into my spirit.

There are hayfields waving,
others turn in the sun,
give up their back-throat bouquet;
Scythes wait for the rhythm of his sweep,
the grace of his stance
reflected in lanky country boys
shirtless at the afternoon roadsides;

There are grease covered hands
lathered with Lava, waiting to dip
into galvanized buckets of spring water,
come up, palms pink,
nails and cuticles smudged and dark.

Somewhere gardens wait at the top of farms
their pale red dirt, dry and anxious for the crunch of hoe,
the dip of spade into potato hills;
Onion patches and cucumber vines
whisper his presence, give up the taste memory,
and I rejoice in the rich yellow offering of peaches.

There are tools expecting to be hung in garages
on pegboards made of plywood and nails;
to be clunked and clanked, used daily
and wiped with the rags of old white undershirts;
Waiting to be borrowed and returned,
borrowed and not returned.

Old songs hang thick in the air each Saturday;
Jeannie and her light brown hair, *Clementine*
and *Buffalo Gals*, come 'round the mountains
and drop from tenor voices.
Tunes which glide and hum unexpectedly,
enter my mind with the turn of morning light.

Water and weeds, packs of plumb unfiltered cigarettes;
Bicycles, wagons, wheelbarrows, posthole diggers,
linoleum, doors and windows moved so pianos
and music can enter the lives of daughters
who wait to write over and over
the story of their life made lucid by his.

No ending to the celebration
passed from his life to mine,
the wisdom of wind, the promises made
in rain and echoed by thunder.
I come to his grave ready to weep
but smile, touch grass and grain,
lift song and thanksgiving into whatever shape
he conjures now, to touch my life.

Deni Naffziger

In the Direction of Words

The nursing home chef prepared
sliced turkey, canned green beans,
boxed mashed potatoes with gravy—
all iridescent under hospital light.
My father hadn't spoken for weeks,
but the day before he died
he was lively.

I fed him little spoonsful
as he nattered on about dead relatives
who'd come to visit that afternoon:
he and his father fixed a reel-to-reel;
while his son-in-law explained
why Federico Fellini mattered.
And Professor Dave,
my mother's father, sat silent
on a wooden chair beside the window—
never answered a single question
my father asked.

Two years earlier,
I'd driven him home from hospital,
following open-chest surgery.
Visors and sunglasses protected
our eyes from snow and more snow
and January light reflecting off drifts
when he told me a secret.

On their honeymoon, my mother cried
after making love for the first time.
She wore flannel pajamas.
Though he made no mention of blood,
I could tell he felt bad about that night.
She had been so unprepared.

Which brings me to my own confession:
after I pulled the spoon through his lips
for what I didn't realize would be the very last time,
I looked out the little metal-framed window,
saw a handful of cars under snow.
I imagined my husband at home
loading wood into the stove, gently
sliding the old dog on the tile floor
away from anywhere ash might land.
I will admit I wanted to leave.
The room smelled like dirty diapers.
Muted on the television, a male dancer
pranced across the black and white screen.
My father was staring at the ceiling again,
his mouth open, his tongue moving
in the direction of words when I stood
to put on my coat, and he asked:
Do I have to go?

Abby Wheeler

River

I have laid eyes on my Ohio nearly every day.
Have seen what it carries, how fast and how high.
Watched the fog burn off in the morning sun and birds
dive for its bugs in still-hot evenings.

I have paddled that river, slept beside it,
cut my feet on its clam shells. Have been diverted by it.
I have sat on a blanket in a crowd and hoped
the fireworks skating on its surface would not end.

Are you from here? My oncologist asks.
The river valley?

Goes on to explain the pulmonary nodules
are common to us born breathing
the musty river air. I'm not surprised,
the way it sinks into dips. How we all have wet basements
that flood when it rains and dehumidifiers to keep old furniture
from rotting. Why not settle into my dark spaces,
seep into unclaimed moments, like grief?

We'll just need to keep an eye on them.
Make sure they don't grow any bigger.

When we were kids and Mom was busy,
Dad would pick up fried chicken
and take us to the river for dinner.
It's been nine months now and we haven't scattered his ashes.
When I close my eyes to talk to him, all I see
is black water. When I close my eyes to talk to God,
I see my father's face. *He must know somethin'*
but don't say nothin', he'd sing.

I try to believe the river lives in the body, steady as a heartbeat
rambling or raging. That we're pinned into place
like a dot on a map. A spot on a scan. A speck of ash.

Anastasia Vassos

Between the Two O's of Ohio

Loneliness
is a short word
on a bicycle.
The road
flatlines west,
the bully wind's
palm pushes
against my chest.

Overhead
the sun shreds
clouds
made of paper
or dry skin.

Mother is missing.
Her memory lies
somewhere
between the two O's
of Ohio.
She lives
in a distant house.

Here
on my bicycle
I pass silence
on both sides
this road that feels
like it could go
on forever.

They have locked
the doors.
I squeeze
down the middle.
For the moment,
I don't look back.

Susan O'Dell Underwood

Etiquette

In Cambridge, I didn't know where to set the etched glassware,
which silver fork was for salad and which for Christmas pie,
or that there was an extra spoon for coffee.
That first married holiday I was terrified
I'd break my mother-in-law's family china.
I felt I seemed to her as backward as I was young.
Those Ohio hills didn't impress me then as kin
to the Tennessee hills I came from.

Decades later, at her eightieth birthday, I led the surprises,
I situated the tiara on her head, served cake,
loved everyone she'd given birth to, took my place
in the huge family photo at the top of the hill.

She and I had dwelt in curves that always seemed
to want to wreck and mangle more than merge.
We'd climbed together for the view of funerals
and weddings and birthdays—all behind us,
all the foregone days in shafts of light
like a shattering kaleidoscope until at some point
the gleaming bits fell into focus.
At that reunion, I came to see myself
the way she did, a woman she called "daughter,"
transformed into a pearl around the bitter grain
of feeling "other,"—*yokel, simple, hick, unworthy*—
I'd sensed I was those years before.

After cake, through nostalgic neighborhoods,
my mother-in-law wanted to see
one last time her childhood home, the one
her father built with his own hands, in the thick
of town wound spiraling into heights.
I teased her then, that I'd never known before
that she was a hillbilly too!
For a second, I thought I'd overstepped until
she nodded and laughed with that wary dignity

of a working-class daughter.
She looked me in the eye as one of her own
and told me that's what others had called her
when she'd moved to Columbus as a newlywed,
spectacular china packed in boxes,
still un-chipped then, every piece whole
with its perfect silver rim, with something to prove.

Jonie McIntire

Blue Light

She wasn't always good with the locks,
said she had to call one of the drivers
to help unload the boxes from the truck.

This was my first day, first job back home
for summer from university—
Kmart, just to pick up hours.

It was a hook lock on a pivot.
Pull this back, flip that here and you could
use a thick strap to throw the door up and open.

She had already shown me how to fuss over
the toiletries and paper goods, to spin everything
forward, label out—customers like it pretty.

As assistant manager, she got a dollar more
and had waited five years to get here.
By the time we got to the truck, I already knew

about her kids, how the old manager kept
stealing and no one believed her until
he got caught on tape and now that extra dollar

sure makes lay away easier because she's
already socking it, didn't tell a soul—paying
cash for that PlayStation for Christmas.

As I worked the lock on yet another truck,
she stood back and studied me—said *damn,
don't doors just fly open for you.*

And sure as shit, they all did.

Jonie McIntire

Our Love Is a Backyard Rosebush

When we moved in,
the rose bush was already here.
A tall frail thing at the very back,
a fence-line peacemaker with the neighbors.

Most years, it barely put out a single bloom.
Japanese beetles made lace of its leaves.
Aphids scarred the tender peachy petals.
The kids with their dodgeballs, softballs, frisbees,
snapped it so often we doubted it could survive.

Through the years you were out of work.
When we lost the baby, then your father, my
grandfather, when we almost gave up on
everything. Through the gracious training of stray dogs
who were also drawn to the rosebush,
a perfect place to piss. Until now,

twenty years later, a summer full of one
gorgeous bloom after another, slowing
into September, even as the petals start to drop,
they smell so fragile, so very sweet.

Holli Rainwater

Walking Down Main Street after Reading
The Elegance of the Hedgehog

*"The Journal of the Movement of the World will be devoted,
therefore, to the movement of people, bodies, or even . . .
things, and finding whatever is beautiful enough to
give life meaning."*–Paloma Josse

Walking down Main Street the other day,
I noticed a barber in his shop
brushing stray hairs from his customer's neck.
He performed the movement with a flourish—
like I imagine an artist signing her name
to a painting that pleases her.
And he was laughing as he did it,
as if the end of the haircut was punctuated
by the punch line of a good joke.

> *the smell of witch hazel*
> *when the door opens*
> *a tinkling bell*

His movement and his laughter caused me to stop for a moment,
to bask in the afterglow of a job well done.
How many hundreds of necks has he brushed?
How many jokes has he heard?
But he seemed so present to *this* neck and *this* joke,
as if he had all the time in the world and could think of no place
he'd rather be than in his orderly and well-lit shop.

> *basement apartment*
> *a sunflower stuck*
> *in a Sun Drop bottle*

As I paused, another movement caught my eye.
The dry leaves at my feet were swirling on the sidewalk
with the same flourish as the barber's brush.
And then the most amazing movement of all.
My scattered thoughts folded their wings and came to rest.

They had been off in another place,
fluttering among pandemics and world peace
and what to fix for dinner.

> *autumn wind*
> *leafing through*
> *a stack of books*

The Way of Consonance, Paloma. Just like you said.
When everything comes together in harmony.
Like when a dancer, after all those hours of rehearsal,
is finally in perfect sync with the music but neither she
nor the audience is quite aware of it until
the movement stops and the music ends
and all that's left is silence
and the beating of hearts.

> *approaching siren*
> *a rose petal drops*
> *to the counter*

Later that evening, as I made soup for my family,
I practiced holding the wooden spoon
with the confidence and presence
of a painter or a barber holding a brush,
and as I stirred, I paid attention to the smells, colors, and textures—
not wishing to be someplace else or to get on to the next thing.
And I wondered if this would cause leaves to swirl outside my window.
And I wondered whether my neighbor,
who might be walking past at that moment,
would stop and notice the swirling leaves
and whether she might feel, not quite knowing why,
like dancing.

> *sparrow*
> *here on the sidewalk*
> *where we both landed*

Penelope Moffet

Walking Away

We were walking away
from a concert hall
where we'd just listened
to Bach or Brahms or Beethoven,
our small family moving
through the Ohio night
when my mother, lit up
from the music, lilted out
some echo of the violins
and threw her arm around me.
Immediately I slipped away,
left her embracing air
until my elder sister
stepped in, hugged her back.
I was 12, embarrassed and repulsed.
How could I know the shrugging off
would stay so many years, rise up
when I think of her who
loved me, loved us,
and is gone?

Penelope Moffet

What Snakes and Fish Recall

fish draw the drifting world
into their senses
green algae
ferns
fallen leaves
currents sweep through them

and snakes in long grass
know much about flesh in motion
bellies flat on sun-warmed mud
sometimes rest triangular heads
among cool blades
forked tongues tasting
what cows eat
ladybirds
rolled sowbugs

in back woods tarantulas
pock fields with holes
rustle about
dreamless weavers practicing
in subterranean haunt
the gift of fur to fur
moving above ground moonless nights
to taste stalks of grass
flowers
spiders' legs

knowing
what those who follow
earth's pull
know

what snakes and fish recall
with each tangled hiss
each splash

Patricia Thrushart

Sojourner Truth Speaks in Ohio
—As told by William Hayward in a letter to William Garrison, 1858

"We should keep things going while things are stirring."

I am the truth-speaker come to Ohio,
pleading the plight of women,
the plight of the slave—
I am God-called.

     "Truth is powerful and it prevails."

You accuse me of being a man,
betrayed by strength and height
and eloquence— and want proof
of my womanhood.

     "I will shake every place I go to."

Here are the black breasts
that suckled many a white baby —
who grew
more manly than you—
while my own lay hungry.

Look now,
to your lasting shame
and my everlasting
resolve.

Kelsey Brown

The Boonies

The speakers in my car don't work as well as they used to,
so the podcasters' voices come through muffled, trapped in water,
or maybe hushed by a small pile of leaves left under the hood
by a cold, opportunistic squirrel in the height of winter.
I'm on my way to something important, something
. . . timely, maybe? Something an hour away by backroads;
the four-lane highway ended one podcast ago.

I pass by a little blue church dotted with tufts of grass,
solitary along the side of the road,
with a singular, broken parking lot, cracks outlining
places to park more clearly than the decaying paint.
The letterboard at the edge of the lot reads:
Concealed Carry Class
        Thursday

The palette of a false Ohio spring is coarse,
dry brushed with tans and weak greens, quiet under
the warm afternoon sun.
Rolling farmlands melt into beds for giants, who sit
upon either side of the highway, passing judgement
as I glide between them,
landscape freckled with dark cows,
bathing in the sunlight of March.

Scott Woods

Day Of the Dead at Bushman's Carryout

I am black and this carryout ain't
so conversely every day is a day of the dead.

We celebrate it by not covering ourselves,
beaming brightly into security cameras
perched behind counters, vultures with a job,
imploring us to smile, as if that were the photo
they'd show on the evening news if this juice run goes south.
We celebrate by keeping things as real as possible,
scratching only where we itch today,
showing only the teeth we've paid for,
a grill we cook only gold smiles on.

It is the day of the dead again
But do you know black people invented the gig economy?
And the girl with the Kendrick tattoo is not
a computer hacker unless you count that autumn
when she bought a cracked firestick in the parking lot
and dropped every spoiler for everything for two months.
All the dollars pinned to her string-top are a wish.
She could buy all the candles in this store
with a bouquet like that if they sold them.
A store that doesn't sell candles in a place
where the lights go out every fifteenth has
trouble on its mind. A beaming halo of bullshits.
You slide her that one you were saving to be a Now & Later king.
You have no idea who she is spreading wide across her hips
or mourning, or both.

It is the day of the dead again
and make way for the delivery driver's dolly
and the wino and the scratch-off posse
in their work uniforms and already smelling of six o'clock.
Make way for skipping school sex and fake summer nights.
Make way for a petition to get this close to your job and
telling everyone in the store to hold up

while you call off work from next door.
And the parade honors that:
no cash register ding
no across the aisle testimony
no whining child who don't know what's at stake here.

It is the day of the dead again
and he has found it.
Discovered it, really, for it was only a legend
whispered about on every block for two miles
amidst a rainbow of gang colors.
He holds it up to the light.
All gasp and dammmmmmn and fist pump.
He has found the bag of Zapp's Voodoo chips behind
the Grippos that even the owner,
for all his forgetful aisle-dancing we know is not a dance,
did not know was there.
And oh, he talks about how he will pay the extra
twenty five cents to take it home,
caresses it in his palm, a child made of chip dust,
and for a moment,
on this day,
which is really like every other day,
we celebrate him from the bottom of our hearts
and our pockets and our memories
of what a dusty spell tastes like
as he stumbles out the door,
then lash him across his back
for the cheap booze with which
he will wash down such glorious sand.

Connie Green

The Worker's Story

One a.m. and I've just come off the evening shift,
everyone I know asleep in bed except my working
companions. Steam rises behind us as we board
the bus back to town, the plant a giant that seems
still only from the outside—cauldrons and motors
rumbling and roaring, the eternal processes running
around the clock, other men and women
there now to keep the beast breathing.

I'm off to bed, will crawl in beside my wife, the feel
of her hip against mine what is left of those years
when desire drove us like pistons, our young daughters
asleep in the next room, the house a universe unto itself,
rising and falling through the long night while
the Milky Way lays its road across the heavens.

Susan F. Glassmeyer

Sears Is Closing

Mrs. Hart, the only mom on our block who worked outside
the home back then, catalogued orders at the local Sears.

What Mr. Hart did was unclear. Gloomy and peripheral, he
came and went unnoticed. Their brood gallivanted coatless

during the cold months. Our mom wondered why they never got
sick, we fought things off all winter long. Still, we grew hardy

once the trees leafed out. Now that Sears is closing, I think back
to that fall day. All of us kids at school just a short walk away.

Mrs. Hart plodding at the store, counting inventory. Mr. Hart,
down the street from our house, in the upstairs bathroom slitting

his wrists. Our mother braved the gruesome scene that day,
scrubbed the red room clean before the Harts came home again.

Karen Schubert

Like worker ants

we scavenge lumber, nails, roofing tile,
an unraveling rug, cracked window.
My garage makes the back wall.

It's 2-story with a dirt floor,
but we want to be upstairs,
heave ourselves through the door

like seals onto ice. The kerosene
lantern stinks. Small kids aren't strong
enough to open the deadbolt

but we let them in after us.
No one can tell we're in there
unless we howl with laughter.

A girl from school drives by
with her dad, sees black smoke.
Mom backs our car out

but Craig's family is visiting Ohio,
new Buick trapped in the shared garage.
Firefighters break the fort into pieces,

kids watch from Scott's yard,
asking each other What happened?
thinking They'll never let us do it again.

Larry Smith

Paddy's Diner

Don't tell me it's just about the cooking,
and swallow that "greasy spoon" talk.
It's a diner, for Pete's sake.
Everybody knows that.

You go there for the breakfast special
bacon and eggs with a stack and toast,
all served with coffee and conversation,
by a waitress who calls you Sweetie and Hon.
The crowd changes, maybe neighbors,
maybe people you went to high school with.
If there's time, Joe, the owner-cook,
comes out to ask how's everything
and how're your brother or sister getting along.

Okay, the dinners aren't the best,
except for Joe's fish on Fridays,
and Marie's meatloaf on Sundays,
and Bertha serving beef tips
and noodles—anytime.
You learn what to ask for,
and you always leave a tip,
in bills and no small change.

Late at night folks out drinking
show up for a steaming plate
of French fries and gravy, sparked
with hot sauce or ketchup.

Marie's mother makes those pies and
those glazed Sunday donuts.
Call it what you want. I know
railroaders and truckers name it
a little piece of heaven.

Mark Youssef

At the Flea Market

Old army coat,
a mannequin torso.
Nineteen fifties chairs,
a set of three.
Tables of rusty wrenches,
old fishing reels,
milk crates
in the dust.
Under the truss,
Fenton glass flutes.
Planters in green,
orange, yellow.
Sweaty families
switch hand the ornaments,
closely inspected against
inner catalogues.
Vendors call out,
sweet and salty kettle corn.
Soft serve.
Relish burgers.
Deep fried anything.
I leave with an old tool box.
My niece
a drusy geode.
Sometimes uncertainty
is all that's left.

Mark Youssef

Forgotten Ohio

A golden summer day, late—
driving the broken and lunging
back country roads.

Windows open,
field aromatics swirl
across our faces.

Seven ravens,
perched on adjacent fence posts.
A deer stands tall
in the meadow.

The pop-up camper
lingers
in the shoulder high grass.
Its top gently baying and frayed,
lacy in the twilight.

Exposed poles rust-frozen
like arms in curtsy,
awaiting a final dance.

Joshua Butts

The Rural Imagination of Landscape & Genre
–after two paintings by Julie Taggart

There should be a book about these lawns.
You know the ones that run right into trees,
a tangle of yards. A poem or a fiction.
An auditor might make sense of them—

you know the ones that run right into trees
with property records might do just as well.
An auditor might make sense of them.
A grave is kind of like living in a house too.

With property records you might do just as well.
Maybe there's a Gravely tractor under a tree—
a grave is kind of like living in a house too.
This painter chooses to paint the tractor head on.

Maybe there's a Gravely tractor under a tree—
red parts, a waddle of knobs & levers.
This painter chooses to paint them from the side,
sort of asking, Do you see the tree or the tractor?

Red parts, a waddle of knobs & levers—
does ephemeral mean not here, here a little,
sort of asking, Do you see the tree or the tractor?
Like asking, Was anyone from here ever famous?

Does ephemeral mean not here, here a little?
No woman lived here last name Copernicus.
(Was anyone from here ever famous?)
She didn't sight-in your gun, let you hunt her land.

No woman lived here last name Copernicus.
This isn't a play & should never be.
She didn't sight-in your gun, let you hunt her land.
An act where you only need a few houses.

This isn't a play & should never be.
Don't put it on right there on the lawn.
An act where you only need a few houses—
since a house provides cover for the interior life.

Don't put it on right there on the lawn—
a dance scene, so puritanical—
since a house provides cover for the interior life
& the television unloads light into the air.

A dance scene, so puritanical!
Somewhere near the middle of the year
the television unloads light into the air.
At this moment small cooking sears sausage.

Somewhere near the middle of the year
there should be a book about these lawns.
At this moment small cooking boils eggs.
A tangle of yards—a poem or a fiction?

Rikki Santer

Idora Park; Youngstown, Ohio (1899-2001)

At the end of a trolly line, a century turns
and the most perfect name for an amusement park takes root
in land destined for the language of twirl and twaddle.
Damp shoulders sway in the open-air ballroom, tongues swirl
in dark tunnels—a nest for boxy boats. Roller coaster *Jack
Rabbit* sometimes runs in reverse—the *Back Wabbit.*
And on a lilting carousel, a cotillion of carved horses rises
likes waves, each mane more erotic than the last.
Logic takes giddy vacation
in *Laffin Lena's* fun house, proud bruises brighten
on manic, bumper-car parades. In this park, gear grease
glistens in an empire of interlocking days.
Then came the fires. '84. A welding torch ignited inside
The Lost River. '86. The northwest quadrant in flames.
'01. The ballroom extinguished.
Mt city's sad trilogy, then the wooden spines
of *Wild Cat* and *Jack Rabbit* bulldozed
for the currency of grass.
These days, the carousel,
pillaged and refurbished for a Brooklyn gallery,
gleams impotent and mute—
a Pentecostal congregation plots for the emptied land,
their future *City of God*—
and in postmortem, dot org merchandise prevails:
I adore the logos on thongs,
the logos on coffee mugs,
the logos on tiny shirts for dogs.

Rikki Santer

Lunatics in Ohio
–Athens Lunatic Asylum (1874-1993)

They buttered judgment, county physicians and judges—
insanity, a slippery cat. By horse or wagon or through
the dusty rowdiness of small-town train depot, patients
transpired. Some with family, some in strait-jackets—
how to decipher a Victorian rubric overlooking the Hocking
Valley where the glacier finally stopped—a healing temple
with drifts of magenta flower heads and Adena ghosts.

Imagine so many protagonists at windows with mandala grills,
moths nibble in closets, grand fountain harbors a summer
alligator—powerful muscle with beach glass eyes. Spoons
wander in bowls of mutton stew, chrysanthemums prideful
in the greenhouse, outings at a natural spring, violins
in the ballroom, then sleep in wings where clocks keep
watch over the musk of sorrow, cotton of surrender.

Ancestor squirrels still stir these thick woods, turkey vultures
nest in weathered eaves, stone wall here, old apple tree there,
dusty casebooks with footprints of enrolled sufferers—
chaotic mixture of epileptics, discarded elders with dementia,
shell-shocked soldiers, tramps as nuisance, violent criminals,
mothers with menstrual derangement, chronic masturbators,
defeated suiciders who aimed at hanging or swallowed pins.

Some say phantoms roam these decaying halls and the cemetery
of weary headstones, many bearing lone ID numbers.
On the floor of an upstairs room, the stain of a woman's corpse
evaporates and returns. Imagine the mounting stigma
of overcrowding, experiments in electroshock, freezing
water baths, lobotomies with ice picks—to not forget
almost a century of jacks-in-the-box, stuffed in tightly
with trembling tally marks on their walls.

Rita Coleman

Our Road

has no single stripe of yellow
painted on its wavy surface,
a sheeting of tar
over a layer of tiny gravels,
a road so old it soft angles
90 degrees
rather than split farmland,
a mere mile end to end
an opening for two state routes,
the dead end for a switch road
near a stop on the Underground Railroad.

Our road curves and rises
in front of our house,
surprising city college
students (who sever a fence,
land in a llama pasture),
a deputy sheriff who swerves
for a deer (he says),
cuts tracks, throws mud,
demolishes a mailbox,
and rams the thick silver maple
that sprung up when hunters
aimed arrows at rabbits and deer.

Our road cuts through 1200 acres,
dips and upslopes
thick with ghost woods
singing at night
in fog-layered mist,
thick with howls
of songdogs and coydogs,
loners and pack,
thick with frontier,
parlayed into corn,
soybeans, cattle pasture,
dreams ancient and new.

Louise Robertson

Climate Change Elegy

Safe Ohio. Easy
Ohio. Green Ohio.
Tropical Ohio. Soft
Ohio. Before it was Ohio
Ohio. People travelled
through here Ohio.
Beavers big as
Volkswagens Ohio.
Used to be 90 percent
forest Ohio. There should be more
moths Ohio. Where
are all the butterflies Ohio.
This is too safe
Ohio. This is too easy Ohio.
This is too green,
soft, tropical, driven,
empty, crowded,
growing Ohio. Used to it Ohio.
Ohio, Ohio. Will be
used-to-
be Ohio.

Barbara McCullough

Out-of-Towners

In the summer of 1993 Bob Denver, of *Gilligan's Island* fame,
came to Marietta to promote his new book *Gilligan, Maynard and Me.*

Above, a yellow-bodied biplane brushes its shadow
over the gathering crowd.
To my right, a tattooed mother, hair pinked and shaved
to her crown, cranes her neck, sure to be discovered,
a ruffled toddler bright against her dirty feet.
Across my path, Junior Miss Interstate 1993, tiaraed
and gowned in late August heat, sashays through,
her brother blaring his ties, "…in case she becomes
Miss America!" In the late afternoon shade,
Mel's Ford's toupee blends seasonably well with
his business suit. Rheumy eyes flash Mel's Diamond House
—40% off every day!
To my left, Norma, heavy at the hip with a lavendered-bowed
baby, smacks her tired boy in blue. Too long on the hot asphalt,
Waiting . . . for what? He wants to be held, too.

She snatches his hand, ping-pongs him across the street.
Hisses, "You always mess things up for me!"
The gap left by Norma's departure opens on two heavily-ringed
women posed under sunhat brims and behind shades,
nodding briefly, first in one direction and then another,
murmuring each other's names. "Myrna," the one purrs
to her companion, "real Appalachians, sweetie."

Kevin LeMaster

Toll Takers 1972

From the road, you can no longer see
the hut where the old men stayed when

there was nothing to do, no more cars
would pull up slow to the lowered gate,

no one waited to press the small tan and
red ticket into a willing withered palm, just

to gain entrance to the tall steel framed bridge that
spanned the Ohio. They would dress in their white tee

and suspenders, wreathed

in thick gray smoke from their black bowled pipes,
chatting about Rainbow Trout biting up river,

the steady growth of their grandchildren and
modernization; a time when they would

no longer be useful, a time when bridges
would be free access and patrons could

come and go as they please. I can see them
laughing at its absurdity, some spitting tobacco juice

into a spittoon on the floor next to them, others clutching
their pipes for dear life, like holding the past in

their bare hands.

Stephanie Kendrick

Closed Road Ahead

The road is crumbling
in the center of town.
Promises of a sinkhole
elate the children, propel them
to chatter of the center of Earth,
mysteries that widen their eyes—
tiny, globed galaxies
lightyears away.
They have been warned
stars sting to the touch and
all we are, was already in space anyway.
So they race to the center of town
and dance
in the soup-bowl asphalt, hungry
for everything in the whole world
to prove to everyone else
that even down here
is just as empty,

and just as vast.

Stephanie Kendrick

Mammaw Comes Back a Cardinal

She visits at the window
while I wash yesterday's dishes,
my hands as wrinkled as hers
before she grew into her wings.
This is the longest
we've been together
without *Days of Our Lives*,
or other scripted sermons
filling the silence
of the decades between us.
She is still as gray and sings
her own songs of faith
that entice even the worms
who have burrowed the deepest.

I still can't land the harmony,
but try to find the pitch,
even now, knowing full well
her songs
were never meant for me.

Roberta Schultz

Rock Pile

I hurt when I first see the slabs,
some as long as human bodies,
unearthed by the power company
as they dig up our old gas line.

A massive pile of limestone erupts
the smooth plane of the dried lakebed.
Like shattered bone through skin, it juts
in jagged angles, painful to see
painful to consider.

They drill and doze for days,
shaking the hill with machines
that resemble giant mosquitos,
yellow proboscises suck into soil
tube fresh veins for new pipe.

I hurt less now that vines and fleabane
reclaim the rocks back into landscape.
A company man comes to halt the dig.
Wires crossed, he says. *Some confusion.*
We've decided to abandon this pipeline.

Never an apology. Never an explanation.
I learn from the earth how to cover wounds,
bind them tight in fast-growing tangle,
soothe broken skin with a poultice of berries.

Preston Martin

Twilight Flight

The yellow crop duster
sneaks up behind as we unwind
another day on the porch.
The engine screams as the nervous plane zips above,
nearly clips power lines,
swoops like another bird of prey to lay a cloud of mist
on soybeans rows lining Petit's long field.
It arches its back at row's end, circles in noisy view
zeroing next pass—
by now we're in the yard, Mary Lou and me,
Bill and Marian, who stopped to tell us
the mill will close.
On the duster's third pass,
all necks swivel as one. It clears wires even closer
to swan dive the beans.
One more fly-by, the engine sings, the plane arcs
and curls into twilight and like that,
I'm in the cockpit over our little town,
I see where Granddad's church burned,
where the school used to be, find Cherry Fork
as darkness closes; leaning south
I straddle the river below Manchester,
Ohio and Kentucky to right and left. I cheer the motor's song,
the giddy lights of Maysville slide beneath,
streaks of colors bob the current,
the stars almost in reach.

Sean Kelbley

Pipeline Surveyors

I resent the men who've come
to mark our land. On breaks they sit

inside their giant pick-up trucks,
engines running so their leather seats

stay hot. Wolf down their Subway
double-meats like puppies vying

to grow biggest fastest. Not yet fully
men: mid-20s, college logos

on their too-clean baseball caps,
Gore-Tex shells un-ripped,

skin paler on the narrow bands
where rings should be. Oklahoma,

Mississippi, Louisiana—not a single
local license plate, and someone here

could use the work. I dislike

their easiness. Their casual bro-nods
when we pass each other on the road,

the way they play the open courts
at City Rec—not bad enough to pity,

not good enough to outright hate.
What kind of guys pound ribboned

stakes, paint arrows red and blue
across a property to show the butchers

where to cut, then just move on?
I've watched them take the measure

of our waitresses at Applebee's.
It's unforgivable, how much

they love their jobs.

Sean Kelbley

There Ain't No Hiding Place*

The road is pocked with black-and-yellow helmets
scraping cautiously across, like soldiers scared
of tripping mines. Some stop, pull up

inside themselves, the way my cousin Kyle retreated
to his parents' basement after graduation. A turtle
won't go more than half a mile from where it's born

unless it's moved. Senior year, we moved one
from the creek behind our high school, watched it jerk
around the playground frame-by-frame like primitive

Claymation. Then Brady Baker stole it, grabbed
a baseball bat, commanded Kyle to swing.

I don't know if God is Love. When rain brings
turtles out, I swerve—go slow on crests and curves
in case He's Calculus. I picture Kyle, presented

like a boxed-up gift by Uncle Tug to that recruiter,
US Army, in a storefront at Grand Central Mall.
Some kinds of love you don't see coming,

like a package on a road near Baqubah.
There was a sudden *crack*, a short and graceless flight
of broken scutes. A nanosecond maybe, in between,

to scream a word like "home."

*From *One Love/People Get Ready*, Bob Marley & Curtis Mayfield

Phoebe Reeves

All the Roads in Brown County, OH

We stretch our tarry seams in the summer sun, settling
down into winter cracks and ruts, our white and yellow veins
faded into the rough patina of oil stains and long-dead

raccoons, streaked rubber, french fry boxes, plastic
Jack Daniels bottles, all the shredded garbage mowers
spit up on us when they pass. You've grafted us one

on the other until now we ramify endlessly over Round-Up
Ready soy fields, scrub forest, sad barns, scooping
over ungraded hollers and hills, jumping washed out culverts.

You laid us here over the land so you could know it all,
or at least use it all. The land does not love us as you do. It bucks
and swells to shake us off—it cannot not love us as you do—

When the tarring crews pass in August, they lay their burnt
benediction on us. The land groans and subsides, dust
rising from the trails of distant tractors, dust rising from our faces,

dust settling in the chicory and clover that spill from our verges
into fields beyond our reach, dust settling where we are not
and on what we cannot touch.

Phoebe Reeves

Prayer for the Household

Judith, who died in this house, left
two things for us in her pale purple kitchen—
a cross-stitched fridge magnet proclaiming
"A woman's place is in the house,
and she goes there right after work,"
and an unopened pack of Winstons,
which my husband says he keeps on hand
for the end times. Which end times we await
depends on the day—biblical, Mayan, cosmic,
biomedical—but Judith a decade ago lay
in her narrow bed in the slope-roofed room
over the front porch and waited to die.
Sixty years she lived in this house
and left her nicotine skin on all the pink and purple
painted walls. Out of respect for the dead,
I left one plastic rabbit statue in the garden,
but I gave the other eight away.
My garden statue is a fox, half hidden in the primroses.
We painted the kitchen sky blue, covering over
her residency, but we're still using her dishwasher.
We still shower in the pink-tiled bathroom.
Her children's heights are still penned
on the doorframe of the upstairs closet.
Oh Judith, house mother, I've worked ten years
to turn your hydrangeas blue, years of bitter
aluminum at the roots, but they still bloom pink for you.

Kevin Hoskinson

Enlisted Man

I stare again and again at the same photo,
the smooth-faced youth in the army portrait
staring from 1941 in that olive-drab suit,
wedge-cap tilted over Cary Grant eyes
caught in the pop of a Fort Dix flashbulb

black hair even at the temples, corporal's
stripes on the sleeves—the early enlisted man
who answered the call from Monroe County
who once rolled a half-track over dunes in Tunisia
who dodged mortars and grenades running

toward wounded infantrymen. Sometimes
he carried body parts from the bloody sand
raced them groaning on cots to soldiers waiting
with kind red crosses on white sleeve bands
and kinder needles of morphine.
                              I never knew that man.

No. I knew the dented dinner pail on the counter,
the evening undershirt in the recliner,
face locked into the CBS Evening News
with Walter Cronkite, the fitful laugh
that cut the air whenever Archie Bunker

yelled at Meathead. That was you, along with
the Pall Malls heaped in the ashtray, the shaking
hands that clenched the evening newspaper,
the stockpiled words trapped in a stuttering mouth
that never told anyone what the eyes once saw.

Dianne Borsenik

Fall Out

As summer slowly fizzles, autumn's showy waltz
begins its all too brief and duplicitous sway.
Cleveland knows its time is short. Polar vortex
dominates the horizon, a season where wheelbarrow
evolves into snowplow, walking becomes improv.
Forget bare feet and flip-flops; hello, flu.

Goodbyes loom, so this last dance is bittersweet;

hearts grow heavy as a steamy solar romance fades.
Ice and snow will tyrannize for months. Cross-over,
jalopy, sedan, tuner, truck, might as well be umiaq
kiting the Northern waterways. But before leaf-crisp
launches into crust-crunch, fall twirls, *pianissimo,*
moving across the floor of Ohio, away from the sun.

Barbara Marie Minney

Rainbow on the Bathroom Rug: Akron Pride

I've lived a whole lifetime as someone I wasn't.

Wandering through gender-sensitive backcountry,
from the hills and hollers of West Virginia,
the grasslands and cornfields of Ohio,
through Stonewall and Pulse,
making it to Akron

like my Appalachian kinfolk
during the great exodus north
on the hillbilly highway,
looking for a better life
in the rubber factories
of Goodyear, Goodrich, Firestone.

I was searching for something too,
not knowing what it was.

The rainbow appeared suddenly,
the afternoon sun's reflection on
the bathroom rug,
a sign that

I had chased the rainbow logic,
revealing myself
on the other side,
more treasured than any
pot of Leprechaun gold.

Coming together
for one day
celebrating our diversity,
letting the world know
we have survived another year,
we are still here,
we are not going away,

a chance to rejoice in my uniqueness,
a chance to cry

a sacred experience
like a dream sequence
fading into misty haze
the crowd cheering for
the choices I have made.
I may have wandered through
a lifetime
as someone I wasn't,
now in whatever time I have left,
I'm home.

Ace Boggess

Landfill Burning

I chose *chthonic*—a good two-dollar word,
as my dad would say, one I had just learned
reading the dictionary. My first year as reporter
at the Huntington newspaper, early 90s.
Morning phone call: *Urgent. Landfill burning
in Ironton, as much as the length of a football field
below the surface. Crews working to snuff it.*

A staff photographer driving, off the two of us went,
crossing the river into Ohio, racing toward disaster
as though four extra feet were needed
to stamp out the flames
though my job was to fill more pages to feed them.

We saw columns of dense smoke rising
like bomb blasts or three tornados frozen in place.
We tasted the stench: rubber & chemicals,
hair & mud. I expected rot from so much waste,
didn't know it could be worse when lit—
a chance to use my newfound word
for *belonging to the underworld.*

How young I was. Naïve. Now, thirty years older,
a different man in a different uniform,
I still can't get the scent out of my clothes.

Ivars Balkits

Auto Lament

O, woe is motor me. O, electric circuit failure. O, dust from the road. O, doors that won't open and windows that won't close. O, worn out tires is me. O, red fluid, o, black, o, yellow going brown. O, rust underneath and corrosion in the behavior. O, tired out, bled out. O, belief and hope stalled by the side of the road. O, panic about the transport. O, persecuted motorist and traveler. O, loss of mobility and free impulse. O, knee jerk reaction. O, anger in the teeth, in the curses and thrown tools. O, man that has no sight forward. O, disturbed dreams. O, the nasty sputum spew of self-castigation from my skin to the planet's.

Lee Boyle

Ohio Explorations

Here is our shared mind,
journeyers' collaged sets.
We are not cooler-troughed
sandwiches at mammoth gas
stations, greyed dandelions
on winding hills navigated,
the swarming campus' night
spirit, graveyards on bricked
fringes of college towns. We
are not them, but have
consumed all, grappling
at mysteries in alley cracks,
mugs briefly gleaming
from tavern panes,
as we pass.

Ellen Austin-Li

Ohio Song

I pressed my head against the plane window
as we passed Boston's Custom House tower.
My last view: clock hands at a standstill. I flew

to Ohio—followed my love far, though
back then, he wasn't so sure he wanted me.
This frontier he had no interest entering.

To me, ensconced in the Northeast, Ohio
seemed a foreign land. But I was carried
to Ohio against the jet stream. Unmarried,

my time for a child nearly expired, I stood suspended
on the bridge over the Old Ohio. The Queen
City on one side, Kentucky on the other. Where

the North meets the South, where slaves swam
to freedom. Where the steamboats' Tall Stacks
replaced the Tall Ships in Boston Harbor,

clambakes traded for barbecue. Cue the sons,
because where your babies are born becomes
home, and I sensed the stirrings of my first one

a few months after I'd moved. I swung in Burnett
Woods like a little girl when I learned the news,
hands gripping the chain link, legs pumping,

eyes fixed on the sky. So high. Yes, I was.
Sailing through the air, I swear I was carried
above Ohio, hung up on this dream.

Tom Barlow

Tedium, or Cambridge, Ohio

Eight years old in 1958 / again condemned by his
parents to three weeks with great-grandmother Birdie
and great-grandad Ray / Cambridge, Ohio,

sixty miles from home in the stone silence that the
elderly wrap themselves in to cushion their weary bones /
no television / no games / no playmates / no coins

for the ice cream truck / only the necrotic hours
between breakfast and bed with the iron water
from the well and trips to the wasp-riddled outhouse /

Birdie puts up her pickles and Ray's rocker wears
grooves in the porch / while the boy stares through
the Cambridge Glass pencil holder on the desk, eager

to see the old house warp and stretch like some magic
has entered and will turn his world into a wonderland
with children his age and monkey bars and ponies

and most of all, glorious noise / and the new day
will open like the fist of his great-grandfather to
show the quarter that has been hidden there all along.

Alan Cohen

Ripening, Harvest, Reaping

Morning's silence softly shattered by dropping acorns
announcing an end while promising beginning.

Chlorophyll gone, the twisting blaze of poison ivy
winds around trees, white berries hidden by the fiery light.
Inside a germ of life to carry swarming
finches through winter's dark.

Wild cherry taken by waxwings, flying gluttons,
gulping purple jewels.
In spring each couple passes a fruit to their mate
in a two step dance kindling excitement for starting anew.
Harvesting now the means of going on.

Day slips to dusk as small persimmon moons
call coons and possums to a feast.
Waddling off to drop astringent seeds is payment for this meal.

Crunching leaves underfoot, my lover and I head for the clearing,
grace notes of katydids bubble up from background cricket drone.
Sweep of Milky Way. Pegasus soaring across the sky.
Our eyes begin the practiced waltz—
A mnemonic counting, 1,2,3 – 1,2,3
to find Andromeda, still chained to her rock.

We cannot see her directly, this fuzzy glow eon-miles away,
but must avert our glance for a magical glimpse,
revealing that which hides, as the poison ivy's berries,
behind a surface gleam.
Something deeper and richer,
a doorway to unknown possibility.

Boom of the barred owl crosses the hollow,
Asking, "Who cooks for you?"
And I hear him say, "What nourishes you?"
And I know it is moments like this, our hands locked together,

sweet smell of harvesting ripeness.
Call of the screech owl, hairs rising on our necks.

Some tribes say the owl calls your name,
announcing the reaper's steps.
May he come when I too am ripe,
ready to give myself back to the world.

Robert DeMott

In Southeastern Ohio Cardinals are the Only Bird of Christmas
–for all my beloveds

Afternoon of another waning year,
with dusk coming early and deepening fast,
my love and I trimmed front porch greens,
hung cheery lights and gaily striped ribbons,
put up our share of bright bows and lacy tinsel,
draped our Christmas tree with shiny doo-dads
stored in our attic since last time, all the while
caroling giddily as we decked our halls in finery,
fal al la, we sang, *fal la lal, h.* . . .
Then, just when we could not imagine more joy,
hosannas of birds—that's the right phrase, I hope—
chickadees, juncos, nuthatches, wrens, and robins,
a whole gang of sprightly denizens,
swooshed in from nearby woods and fields
to feast on winter's banquet at our yard's edge:
scarlet holly berries, blue-black pearls of sour gum,
and those clustered morsels of bittersweet,
tiny orange globes shedding fractal light
on Northern cardinals, birds of soulful folklore,
visiting spirits of those we once loved and lost,
ornaments now gracing bare limbs and shrubs,
there among fruitfall and a dust of snow.

Jeff Gundy

Reports from an Interior Province

1. SOME DECEMBER

It all begins when everything seems dead,
bald cypress finally plucked clean, empty bottle

tossed in the weeds, muddy water escaping
under the bridge. Time like a locked door,

like a broken shingle, like an old friend
vanished halfway through the chorus.

The county's last ring-necked pheasant,
plodding down the waterway, calling for a mate.

The broken stalks exhausted in the fields,
barely breathing, waiting for the test results,

sick to their hollow bones. The vast
March moon, distant and stony

and clean, and not looking down upon us,
not looking anywhere at all.

2. THE GREAT PURE DAZZLE

Some days the light is just too much, blasting the tender
new leaves of the linden, even here where not much attention

gets paid. Being ignored is privilege, as it's taken me years
to understand. I was a straight white country kid

with plenty to eat and pretty good parents and only
the prospects of nuclear annihilation, an eternity

of fiery torment, and stochastic bullying to trouble my nights.
Some mornings the light was too much, winter days

with the snow a great pure dazzle. Some days I hid my eyes.
Some days I stared too long at the girls as they blossomed

and preened, preened and blossomed, all of us
baffled by their new powers. I learned to sweat,

to run hard one way, turn, lean and wait for the whistle
and run hard back. Some days I got home after dark,

empty as a new wineskin, sore and weary, still all
the chores to do before we could crowd around the table.

3. THE NEW KNEE

We judge our neighbors by how well
they clear their walks and driveways,
with minor allowances for those
who live on corner lots, or alone.

B. raps at us from his upstairs window,
waves wildly. We wave back, pleased,
we used to meet on Wednesday nights
at the pub downtown, walk home
happy and a little tipsy. How long
since we actually talked?

We grumble across the snow pack,
your new knee tender and stiff,
then choose the street, mostly clear,
empty unless the school kids
and teachers are coming or going.

Don't walk on loose dirt, E. taught me
long ago, it makes it way harder to
shovel it back when you're done.
It's true of snow too, everybody
knows, way better to shovel
when it's fresh. Not much to do
after you drive it flat and icy
but wait for a thaw.

4. EVERY DAY OF FEBRUARY 2021

The forecast is cold, then snow, then colder. M.'s knee
is better every day, a little, she's even done the basement stairs

although she grumbles. And now even the cardinals
have gone dark across their backs and wings. I've tromped

a sort of path to the feeders but it's lumpy and treacherous
as I clamber around the pile at the end of the driveway.

The birds love safflower seed, empty our biggest feeder
in half a day, scatter most of it on the ground where the doves

and squirrels and finches mingle to peck and nibble.
The sparrows in their dozens flock in and out, skittish,

never at rest for long, I wonder how they don't burn
more energy than they can eat. I'm more or less

the same, not in motion but in mind, flitting here
and there, never at rest for long enough to rest.

Jeff Gundy

Seven Ways of Looking at Raspberries

1.
Between the compost pile
and the birdfeeders
there are only the raspberries.

2.
Except for the asparagus,
head high and prickly.
And the vines, volunteer mulberries
and redbuds and maples.
And the thistles. And the ground ivy.

3.
A gardener and his raspberries
are not one.
A gardener and his raspberries and asparagus
and innumerable uncultivated flora and fauna
are one.

4.
The Japanese beetles
suckle the sweet red juice of raspberries
and mate ecstatically among the leaves.

5.
In the dark earth
raspberry runners nuzzle
and murmur all winter.

6.
Every good boy
deserves raspberries
eaten straight from the canes.

7.
At the rate of nine inches a year
the raspberries are marching.

8.
Once there were seven raspberry canes
dug from the friendly preacher's back yard,
carried home in a black plastic bag.

9.
The plum trees behind the raspberries
were released from their earthly bonds
decades ago.

10.
In the same humid morning
an earnest gardener can pick raspberries
and pull thistles
with fair results.

11.
Raspberries do not count,
but they multiply.

12.
There are more than seven ways
of looking at raspberries.

Myrna Stone

Taraxacum Officinale

     Early spring, the first light
still vague, nacreous, glacial
  and nothing of the season in the air
     but rain, the gray and lateral
  sweep of limbs above the roof
a scrawl, a line drawn in spindle and spine—
  nothing of the season in the mire
     of waste place and field
but the wildflower the French call *dent-de-lion*
     for the serrated edges
       of its basal leaves.

     In this light, this moment,
this might be home, my mother
  alive again, in love with the turning
     of the year, down on her knees
  in the fields of the Ohio Valley
to harvest the greens: alchemy of earth, wind,
     and water, a sort of sunlight
       on the tongue,
the walk home somnolent, her work at the sink slow,
     the kitchen tamped down,
       doorway and window.

     The rain falls, now incremental,
measurable across the vertical
  light, the endless pattern already begun
     in the parry of root and knife,
  then the leaves in a moment
darken to bitterness, and the blowball, blowzy
     on the wind, relays desire
       or fidelity promised,
and what remains in the hand—a tally of lapsed
     time—is counted, seed
       by seed, hour by hour.

John C. Mannone

Speculators
–Appalachia during Reconstruction

They wielded the same kind of dirty carpetbags
I saw down South full of dust-filled promises.

What were they planning to do with all the *worthless*
land they'd be taking off my hands? I didn't hear

the scarlet tanagers or the pine warblers
miss the notes in their songs as I signed the papers.

I didn't smell deceit on the ink-and-must stained
documents . . . only the sweet honeysuckle outside.

But soon my ears would burn when I heard
the truth, my mouth left acrid, my tongue stumbling

on the cheap texture of lies. Blinded. I couldn't see
the sun setting behind the grieving mountains—

shadows veiling their purpled faces. River babbling
regret down below. I know it won't wash my sin away.

Just like they swindled us out of our common land—
the rocky wilderness for timber, coal, and tan-bark

with chicanery and fancy laws on *corporate enclosure,*
they'd be digging out the ore; draining gas & oil

and the hearts and minds of simple mountain people.
I should've known when they came in those lawyer suits

wearing those uppity smiles, swinging satchels with their
promise-me-the-moon-but-give-me-the-gutter looks.

Sherry Cook Stanforth

Lost

after the nasty Bradfords shed
white petals and the corn grows

in lines of clothianidin thiamethoxam
glory all rounded up and ready

I walk down to the hive
to break the wax seal

the workers built
to lock out the world

I find that nothing lives
Inside—that I've only come

to grieve a lost tribe of bees
to imagine their buzzing

miraculous potential—how they
once knocked dust from blooms

feeding a hungry world from crib
to coffin, and of course I can't holler

them back to lavender beds
or goldenrod fields where they

know the south-cut paths to home
and the time to beard or ball up

against winter's mean slice
dreaming of seed and purposeful

dancing and the heavy peace
of locust plumes. Red clover

still pearls along the roads waiting
to hold my wandering long gone bees

lid lifted and crowbar flung to weeds
I kneel down to receive my lesson

Anna Egan Smucker

First Day, First Grade, St. Peter's School

Lunch time: no sloppy joe, no milk, no apple,
not even a tray. The girl on the bench beside me
said I must have sat in the Unlucky Place.

No teachers anywhere. The kids around me felt sorry,
but wouldn't share. Tired of sitting hungry, I walked
out of the lunchroom, wanting *never* to return.
I crossed the street, and took the city bus home.

Mother, in the middle of diapering my brother,
called my father, and made a bologna sandwich.
Dad, workday interrupted, returned me to school,
placed me at the end of the after-recess line,
told me I had to stay the whole day.
No one had even noticed I'd left.

For the rest of the year, I brought a sack lunch from home.
I didn't like school. But one day, I *discovered* that letters
made words, and words made stories—stories I could make
myself. Spot could do more than "run, run, run."
Lucky me, I could make *anything* happen. And I did.

James Cochran

There and back, all in one day

Somewhere between
chitchat and heart to heart,
my parents and I
talk in the living room
while toads trill
in the dark pond outside.

We rub each other's feet
as tomcat on the porch
bats at moth come to gaze
in rippled glass
of farmhouse window.

The chemo is tomorrow,
we'll rise before dawn,
leaving the hills for the big city
on its glacial plain,
smooth like the thin white paper
that covers the exam table
like an unblemished shroud,
always a fresh length
awaiting each patient.

Outside the cancer center
there is an artificial creek
with real ducks and ducklings,
a real hawk perched nearby,
waiting for the right moment.

Inside, masked patients wait like ghosts
for port draws and blood test results,
then line up to lie down in poison beds,
putting faith in their bodies and science.

Today the news is good,
blood counts better,

cancer smaller,
so we count our blessings
and head for the hills.

"There and back, all in one day,"
my parents used to announce
upon arriving home from an outing
when I was young.
I repeat those words now to my father,
then switch off the ignition.
We sit a moment in silence
before going in the house.

Kristine Williams

Hollow

Anger like that leaves you hollow,
leaves you open,
which would be ok any other day
except today you are driving and listening
to 80s on 8 on Sirius XM and
of course the Scorpions are singing
about *still loving you*
and your mind pokes at that 40-year-old memory,
like a tongue in a bloody, used-to-be tooth hole,
pain exquisite but you just can't help yourself
and here you are feeling the loss of some long ago not-ending
with a boy you have written at least a dozen poems about
and who, damn you, you still long for
in a way that somehow grows sharper with time
and you want to crank the volume and drive,
backroads where redbuds and dogwood run wild as your thoughts,
maybe wail,
think about what might have tried to but never could have been.
Instead, you turn right off County Road 25, onto Gura Road
and up the hill, around the curve,
peepers in the pond singing their own song
and you know tonight they will be so loud
they will drown out everything else.

Cindy Dubielak

After Depression

No one came around in school
with sign-up sheets for cheerleaders
for the mentally ill, even though
we were Catholics which technically
meant we were Christians. We were
expected to swing our legs over
the side of the beds in our
respective homes, brush our teeth
and brace ourselves for the drama.
As my mother, tired of her own life
reminded me, we were not Lazarus
dead four days waiting for nothing
except our Savior man to show up.
We were privileged. Christ,
even Mrs. O—our teacher in gym—
took her job so seriously we actually learned
how to draw a bow and let loose the arrow.
Who knew all these years later
I'd pick it up again, teach my son
that it's an honorable way to kill?
That he would walk into our home
after the hunt holding the leg of a doe
who had been shot cleanly in the chest
and suffered little. We both cheered that day.
he, for the pleasure of providing food
for our table and me for pride in
the provider.

You want to know what's kept me here?

I don't waste time wondering why
so many people I love step off
the ladder they've climbed with the prayer
of a quick death. Exhaustion is a one-way
street I have traveled. Like water filling
the Titanic, we can only resist so long.

Rising water will take you with it
right to the edge where ocean
meets sidewall and, if you're lucky,
you can step off into the blue before
the perilous suck of the sinking ship
pulls you down. Either way
you are dying. You can choose.

Jane Ann Fuller

To A Suicide in Zanesville, Ohio

–Terry Thompson set free 118 of his exotic
animals before shooting himself in the head.

I don't know what you believe
when you unlock the gate,
unfasten your jeans and take out your privates,
deliver your body to the animals.

But your suicide, the partial undressing, such devotion
to big cats, black bears, the macaque,
make love a lost cause,
the root of all bad ideas.

Nothing can change
how a girl looks in the mirror
of the muddy river, becomes part of the landscape,
aimless, wild. What can I do

but rub my kids' sweaty chests with Vicks,
answer their cries with my cries,
sit on the pony, Red,
when a lion steps out of the shadows?

It's too late when the zookeepers come
in overalls with tranquilizer guns.
Hearts perfect for Zanesville, Ohio.
Plenty of real ammunition.

Jane Ann Fuller

Burning The Orchard

When I was a girl, 9 or 10, like Gretel,
I held in my throat (as long as I could)
the dove's somber coo before rain,
knelt in the tall grass of my father's orchard,
while he set fire to living trees
of *transparent yellow*, thick with tent worms—
this sacrifice would keep the rest
from harm. We doused
with gasoline the cuttings we had piled,
then lit and listened to them burn.
The death cry climbed to such a pitch
it disappeared
with smoke into the stars. We poked
at worms that writhed inside
the charred cocoons. We couldn't
let them live.

****

How does a girl burn? First, she says *good riddance*
to the junipers. To the clouds sitting on the trees
like Buddhas. Black ants
(good-bye to them as well)
who prick the cheeks of peonies.
Then, she razors her head
smooth as nacre. Hair falls like ash
and she breathes oneiric burning.
She multiplies loss (mother, step-mother,
witch) because the past is never finished.

She will survive the truth,
grief being her metronome,
by repeating it.

Embers of her climb
like stars backward
to their constellations as if

they know the way home.
Her eyes already cinders, she belongs
to the night sky's crematorium
where the heart burns last.

Mary Lucille DeBerry

Light and Ring Imagined
–*Ernest Glenn Munn*
Missing 1942—Discovered 2007—Buried 2008

A small yellow light caught the eye of the ice-hiker,
the writer, the journalist, as he visited the mountain site
where he discovered a World War II aviator's body in a glacier.
"A little tree," he first thought, then realized the air was thin
as his Sierra Nevada-affected brain at this high altitude.

A small yellow light, the sun bouncing off something—
something like a ring. No tree could be here, high where
no grass grows. It is a ring, and the ring is on a finger,
the finger of a 23-year-old cadet crashing during a pilot
training mission sixty-five years-of-tears ago.

A small yellow light as bright as the airman's blond hair;
as bright as the hopes of his three sisters now in their 80s
all wearing long-time married names, all living still not many
miles from the Ohio town where they attended school,
not far from where he volunteered for the U.S. Army Air Corps.

A small yellow light, brightened by a hundred candles, glows
behind the coffin, where at either end, military men stand guard.
Men whose grandfathers were contemporaries of this young
airman. The Air Force Academy's cherished poem *High Flight*
is read. His sisters weep. Small yellow lights of faith burn
                                        steadily in their eyes.

Sylvia Freeman

Giraffes

We made a game, my three-year-old and me.
I'd ask *What does the dog say?*
She'd say *Bow-Wow*, get down on all fours
while the puppy wiggled, licked her face.
I'd ask *What does the bear say?*
she'd growl in her deepest voice, box the air with her fists.
If I asked what the giraffe says, she'd laugh
in a high voice yell, *Mute, Mute!*
Then she'd double over with giggles
run into her room, ending the game.

But today, I read that we had it wrong.
Giraffes aren't mute after all.
In a Viennese zoo after the musicians
have packed their instruments for the night
after the vocal arias are silenced—giraffes hum.
Perhaps, strands of Strauss still hang in the air
create longings a creature must respond to.

I wonder if they hum in chorus, in harmony
or only to a lover? Is it serious or playful?
Do they intertwine those elongated necks
move together as in a dance, gather sounds
that reverberate into midnight song?

Once I saw Madame Butterfly in an amphitheater
in the Cincinnati Zoo. Occasional background sounds
African Lion's roar, howling monkeys, laughing hyenas
joined the performance, accentuating Puccini's genius.

Tonight, I tip toe through my daughter's room
tuck a blanket around her smallness
open the window to gardenia's scent
firefly glimmers and nightly chorus
whoo-who of owls, snapping cicada wings
coo of doves, harmonies for her dreams.

In Cincinnati perhaps an elephant sways
his trunk remembering *Un bel de Vedremo*,
while in Vienna, giraffes hum through the night.

Sylvia Freeman

New Way to the River

storm-toppled trees
fallen branches, brambles
webs of leaves and vines
stand between me and river's roar

so many years since my son climbed
hardwoods leaning over the river
found dragonflies in the water
built stone villages on the shore
skipped rocks, sent them
bouncing to the other side.

I can see him still
under the brilliance of fall
collecting red and yellow leaves
or bundled in a winter coat
pointing out patterns in ice puddles
or finding trout lilies, wild ginger
first warm days of spring
or wading in the shallows
watching River Cooters
in deep green heat of summer.

now nothing makes sense
everything out of sequence, out of time
sunlight shimmers through leaves above me
flickers on moss velvet path
where flood waters have been
I pick up a handful of sand
sift it through my fingers
remember the day
we scattered ashes in the river
watched them drift downstream
disappear
into the swirl of an eddy.

Jessica Cory

The Mighty Ohio

I.
The coal
    the coal
        it sinks to the catfish
mouths, shovel and shut, shovel
        and shut, spooning in
rocks and sticks and A-plant runoff.

II.
The barges'
      twisted steel would sell
    well at the Circleville scrap yards,
but it would have to be salvaged

first. My sister took a selfie,
     her shadow lurking like a ghost
  on the murky river's surface. A somber, small reflection
painted in oil and gas. My parents warned us

     not to wade in. I asked if fish
would gobble up my toes, like the 6 footers
    caught in Paint Creek.

III.
Dad chuckled, *There aren't any fish in there, Jess.*
    He used to fix tracks for the C&O. Drove
heavy equipment across the river's bridge spans. Recalls
      barges on fire and smoke like the Cuyahoga up North.

IV.
But the EPA made it a-okay, the local
    newspapers say. And coal keeps the lights on,
as the slogan goes, so nobody cares
        what enters catfish holes.

Terry Focht

Big Turtle Creek

Deep down
in Jackson County,
where Mountains
and Blue Grass meet,
seems there's a creek
around every bend
and old Indian trails
to find your way.

Every summer
Uncle Moss and I
hiked those trails,
scouting for one more
fishin' hole.

Folklore says Daniel Boone walked here.

Cane poles and fishin' knives,
compass and canteen,
sleeping bag and fish stringer,
fresh dug worms and crawdads,
just about all a boy would need.

He taught me how to fish,
to scale and to gut,
attacking my fingers,
fish eggs and guts,
guts and worms,
fresh meat and guts.

"Be careful now,
those catfish will sting ya," he sang,
as I bravely and boldly,
whacked of their heads.

The sun . . . too soon fading,
catfish sizzlin' on a stick,
fresh caught marshmallows,
campfire stories,
imagined calls of native drums and flutes,
of spirit dancers, in rhythm with the earth,
stars living just above the treetops,
dew from the darkening forest
settling on my sunburned skin.

Marjorie Maddox

Branch Rickey: Turkey Creek One-Room Schoolhouse

Seventeen, a farm boy from Duck Run, Branch knew
those school walls housed bullies who spat
tobacco juice in teachers' eyes, then beat them bloody, bruised.
He took the job anyway, stood up, stood firm

within those schoolhouse walls. Bullies who spat
later sat and learned what the hills and river tell:
take the job anyway, stand up, stand firm,
protect the place you love. The young ones who

sit and listen learn later what the hills and river tell—
what you become you pass on.
Protect the place you love. The young ones who
watch stand up for young ones who watch

who you become in Turkey Creek or Duck Run. Who
knows these fields and mountains knows this.
Watch how the younger ones watch you standing up
to bullies. Home remembers your name,

knows how these fields and hills know you.
These country roads are yours. In every town, every ballpark,
name the bullies. Remember your home, your name,
how, at seventeen, just a farm boy from Duck Run, Branch knew

what this country could be, every dirt road, city lot, ballpark.
Robinson deserved to play. Each day, stand up, stand firm.
At seventeen, farm boy from Duck Run, Branch knew
how bullies spit, dig in cleats, bruise skin blacker.

Robinson deserved to play. Watch how he stood up
    for those who watched. Stand firm.
Together, they fought for what they loved. Remember
    your home, their names
till bullies spit, cleats spike, skin bruises blacker a little less.
Use the job. Stand up. Stand firm. Again. Again. Again.

Young ones, fight for the world you love. Remember your home.
Name the hills and rivers, what they tell you of yourself
again and again. Take the hard job. Stand up. Stand firm.
What you become you pass on.

Marjorie Maddox

Those Hills: 1960s

Before backseat seatbelts,
we rode those Hocking Hills

unhindered, my artist-aunt
steering her VW camper

wildly toward each new view
whiplashing us into awe.

Once settled, she painted;
we investigated,

the land a courteous, quiet
guide, leaving us to creek

and our own best devices.
By day, we hiked the trails

of cliff and gorge, waded ankle-
deep across slate where

my "seater fell at Cedar Falls"—
a family joke still repeated.

By night, we camp-fired
our way into legend, the hermit

lore of Old Man's Cave,
the shadows of rock bridges

and hidden trolls and what would
and wouldn't be beyond

the moss and ferns, beyond
those canopies of dream-

like explorations still here
in the brain's rocky terrain,

the twisty map of memory
where, beneath the last

waterfall, we wait for all
our long-ago lost ones,

deep in those dense woods,
those sunlight hills of Hocking.

Barbara Sabol

The Stargazer

–Unknown Flood Victim # 6: Male. Age 14. Light complexion. Regular features . . .
Short, grey knee breeches. Large aquiline nose. Blue eyes. Fine, intelligent,
and pleasing look. No shoes or stockings.*

Huddled on the back porch stoop, I trace
the bright studs of Orion's belt with my finger,
to his sword, then mid-way down,

find the Nebulae: a misty globe of stars—
young stars—that through a reflector telescope
becomes a gleaming reddish swirl.

At tonight's library lecture, the image
of a sixty-minute exposure (imagine!)
showed stars too faint to be seen from earth.
Light years away, the lecturer said. *Light years.*

In that moment my chair lost its hold
on the floorboards. Everything in the hall
blurred, and I felt lifted up and out of my own skin.
Spun like a human nebula.

I can't even describe the feeling. Walking home,
I was still a little wobbly, like that time
I stole a couple swigs from Pop's bottle.

Pop tells me to get my head out of the clouds.
Set my sights on the steel industry, building
railroads, cities. The possibilities, he keeps saying,
are endless.

What ignites me could not be farther
from what he goes on about. His life's given over
to what's dug from the earth—iron ore and coal
deep beneath these mountains.

But far up, above the chimneys and smoke stack fumes
whirling like chalk dust, are whole entire worlds
we don't even know. Endless worlds.

*Morgue entry from Beale's Morgue Book of the Johnstown flood of May, 1889

Barbara Sabol

Summer Along the Stonycreek

From a needle eye in the Alleghenies
this sheet of liquid shimmer
unseams the earth.

Steel rail and forest trail
run alongside, north and west
to the Highlands. At this bend
the current circles, chisels, deepens

for the child's cannonball,
the raccoon's cupped hands,
ribbon snake's undulations,
a polished assembly of stars.

See how the water gathers
oak's shadow, hemlock's needled brush
in its wending,

how the shifting clouds and lift
of broad-winged hawk echo
on its surface.

One with sky, river meets itself
as deluge, thin rain, as mist.

A body could float through time
on its muscled back. Our stories
are ferried in its depths: caravan
of arrowhead, latchkey, crockery, bone.

Listen now to the river's patter, reminding us
Not everything is broken.

Kathleen S. Burgess

The Great Flood
–Ohio River, January-February, 1937

Mice-footed it comes. Then like a plague it
oozes over Portsmouth's floodgates.
                                        Water
infests basements, creeps upstairs.
                                        It soils
food on tables.
                        A man rows streets sheened
silver in surging waves. It's
                                Claude Burgess
taking his family—pregnant wife Pearl and
four-year-old Dick—to high ground in New
Boston.
                She holds a basket of food, toy car,
a change of clothes, dry blankets.
                                        Pearl and
four other pregnant women with children,
sleep on a wood floor.
                                Claude rows sisters,
families, neighbors, many parcels soaked by
deluge.
Sundown:
                        Sore, wet back, arms, hands, feet.
Roiling dreams of mouse-gray water swarm.
Daylight:
                Where is the porch of this house
his father built?
                        Submerged.
                                        The boat, oars
Claude built?
                        Taut rope says the johnboat is
wedged beneath the outdoor steps.
                                        In only
his shorts, he slides into the river,
                                        gasps and
follows the line, wrestles the boat. Uprooted

things bump past, into him.
                              Lungs burn.
                                        Up
for air.
          Underwater he unties the boat.
                                        Climbs
a pier, hauls up, reties his boat.
                              It bucks hard.
He cloaks in blankets.
                              Lights fireplace wood.
Shivers hanging clothes before a fire.
                                        Rows on.
Rows into sleep.
Daylight:
          He helps townfolk out windows, off
roofs. Twelve days of rain.
                              Each night crawls
from hills, thick, feared, like the muck fouling
homes of a million homeless people.
                                        Water
retreats back to its banks.
                              Now flood survivors,
from Pittsburgh to Cairo, begin their search to
save from ruin
                    whatever the Ohio's left them.
She births Jack in the home they have cleaned.
Claude and Pearl leave nothing, no one behind.

Kathleen S. Burgess

The Boy

was two or three years old. He did not talk much.
Collected whatever appealed to him, willy-nilly:
rocks, burnt matchsticks, tabs from beverage cans.

He laid them in lines on bedroom shelves, a front
porch rail, the gravel drive, like any boy collecting
Matchbox cars, action figures, game cards. Mom

opened the kitchen door onto the deck. She saw
him on the walkout patio, little feet, thin legs pale
in dinosaur-print shorts as he flailed a Wiffle bat.

He was pounding something with it. She flew down
steps from the deck, thinking he might be cracking
open a toy or a mouse one of the cats had dragged

home. But the object of his swinging and cudgeling
was a hummingbird. Female. Limp, still in the sun.
How and why he found it, beat it, she couldn't know.

Maybe it had scared him buzzing above his head into
flowers or sky reflected in a glass door. Maybe it fell,
stunned. She knew death took hold often in this way.

Something rubbed along her ankles to make a claim.
Gently, she took the bat from the small boy hands.
He shivered and sweated. His eyes glazed as if

daydreaming. She lifted him, the boy. Carried him
inside. Later she prepared a box for the bird, so that
they might scoop up the still form and place it just so.

Matthew Gilbert

An Occurrence at Meigs Creek
–a poem for Ambrose Bierce

what would it take to remember
where you come from?

after so many wars
inside yourself, it's easy to see
how to lose your tracks

with a book, a story,
those shouting words,
a man who bound his own wrists,

a man who didn't
forget how to battle
at Shiloh and Chickamauga,

the scars
long after they disappeared.
you listened.

we will forever hear the dead child
the soldier, the imaginary
escape from death.

your ghosts will linger.
we will wait for silence of owls,
an echo of the life left behind.

Colby Smith

Grandmother

Entombed six years,
I learned after a botched dinner
she was born in a company town,
still standing, now private property
where desperate addicts squat
until they get booked or shot.
From puberty until she got out,
she'd been a whore,
to get moonshine for her mother,
scrip for her sisters.

I've never been to that ruinous
company town, never seen
the slouching hills, empty mine
shafts, decrepit shacks, dense
holler lined with beech, oak,
willow—verdant skeletons.
I'm a coward, the antithesis
of noble Faustus, spinning yarns
of the dead.

Teagan Hughes

Remnants of a Company Town

Can you feel the earth hollow under your feet?
The air is thick and close and I cling to it like moonlight—
Can you feel the fog in your chest?

I scraped my palms on jagged shale
And my lungs caved in under the blanket of the dark—
There are ghosts in your groundwater and you can blame
the far-off suited men who let the limestone give way over my head.

I hold my lantern against the smoothed stones and
the weeds, grown tall and ragged—
How long has it been, now? How long
have I been trapped under aching ground?

My form scatters in the sun and the night fog dissolves—
Can you feel the earth hollow under your feet?
Can you feel the ghosts in your chest?

Teagan Hughes

Broken Down

i am from the self-contained unit.
broken, yet healing
yet constantly changing.
i am made of the instinct to run;
the natural impulse to get three hours away from here
in a rusted-out oldsmobile.
my people are from wherever they could get by;
from rows of worn and shuttered houses
from where,
if you were being buried alive,
you were handed a shovel
and told to
dig yourself out.

Elizabeth Beck

His Name Was Angel

Opened door Thanksgiving night
for the final time. His mama will
need to move away from holes
shot clear through to walls. Hard
to believe his smart mouth
caught up with him. Yet not.
Just wish it weren't true. Wish
gangs didn't bang. Fourteen
too young to die. Spoken words
cannot be erased when bullets
do the talking in response. Angelic
he does not look, gray-faced
in white casket wearing ill-
fitting suit. I don't even have
the words in Spanish for
my condolences. Look at her
hands instead of her face
creased in grief no mother
should know. Wonder if older
brother sits in church, feeling
guilt pressing down or if he
is plotting revenge. Hope
it doesn't continue. Pray
it ends here. Child in coffin.
My students wailing in pews.
Stench of death lilies. Hands
clutch rosaries. Priest stands
at attention. I do not wait
for the prayers. Push my way
past teachers lined up to pay
respect. Push front door.
Another front door. Lean
against red brick and weep.

Elizabeth Beck

Mother's Day Card Assignment

I don't live with my mom. My mom is dead.
Don't be sad, Ms. B. I got a good granny.

My mama's locked up. My mom's in Mexico.
We may go back this summer. For good. Maybe.
I have a foster mom. Does that count? I live
with my auntie. It's okay 'cept there's too many
damn kids. I sleep on the pull-out sofa. I ain't
got a room. I share a room with my two brothers.
We need a bed. Our house got burned up. Can
I go to Youth Service Center for my bag
for the weekend? I need my food. I don't need
a belt. I'll pull up my pants. Can I go to the restroom?
I just started today. *You know.* We don't have
internet at home. But I got my phone. Is this a real
rock, Ms. B? Where'd you get it? Are these
plants real? My granny grows plants. Sign my
behavior sheet please. I need all three's today.
I lost my pencil. Can I use the hand sanitizer?
Where's the hall pass? I go to grief group today.
Can you read this poem? My daddy got shot.
It's my birthday. I'm turning twelve. We go
to church on Tuesdays. And Sundays. But
mostly Tuesdays. My cast comes off next
week. My daddy gets out next month. We
came across the border. I'm not ashamed
to say it. Can I call my mom? Can I go
to my locker? Who's that in that picture,
Ms. B? Is that your son? Can I write
on the board? Can I at least erase it? Do
you have snacks? Where do you keep
your band-aids? Can I go see the nurse?
This glue stick is all dried up. Can we
use the scissors? When is this card due?

Sarah Robinson

Dead Promises

The largest gift I'd ever received
arrived in a long wooden crate
nailed shut.
Crated in Appalachia,
shipped to sea level,
it sat delivered
out on the Mississippi lawn
mashing down the grass.
"Looks like another dead body."
I'd stood next to a closed casket—
not quite this size—
holding forever
my beloved brother John's drowned remains.

"Your dad shipped us
a grandfather clock?" my husband wondered.
"Let's hope. Remember how
he admired our eleven-foot ceilings?" I sighed.
We pry it open,
relieved to see a stately
mahogany cabinet
with intricate works.
It gets propped up,
leveled on the wood floor in the front parlor.
I give its pendulum
a swing, back-and-forth,
admire the ticks called "Royal"—
one-per-second, like a heartbeat.
How touching from the man
who inflicted wound after wound
on his son's inner works,
to ship *me* a closed-casket gift
with the promise of a heartbeat,
unlike his dead son.

William Jolliff

Still Life With Banjo

One night with a little bit of bourbon
and the house empty, his wife gone away
to the coast (he'd never understood the coast),

he pulled his banjo from beneath the bed
and began to pick his catalog of tunes:
how he missed her but was glad she was gone,

this good job and why he had taken it,
his kind but sophisticated children
with straight teeth and well-worn passports;

then one about graduate school, eight years
of assuming a way of looking at books
that didn't suit how he felt about them

and, as he knows now from watching himself,
could never have fit a kid who showed up
on the land-grant campus at seventeen,

with spackles of crick-mud on his boots,
a Goodwill coat, and two new pairs of jeans,
never having made the ghost of a choice

but recalling a high school teacher's claim
that you need to leave to become somebody,
especially if you have a kind of *gift with texts*—

a promise he'd shown as the boy who didn't
take to tractor work. But his only memory
of feeling whole was when his grandmother,

sitting on the porch of a white frame house
near Magnetic Springs, admiring a fresh line
of blue shirts she'd just scrubbed on a board,

resting half a minute, had picked out a tune
then handed him the banjo and said, *Honey,*
I've an idee you're going to need this,

then took his pale hands in her red ones, said,
Here, put your fingers here. You go ahead.
And so he took it, and he went ahead.

Karen Whittington Nelson

Morning at Ellis Dam

I wake to my father whispering my name
from outside the tent; inside, pale morning light,
firefly green, glows through the worn canvas.
I quickly dress, bent over and careful, so not to send
melting stars dripping through pinpricks
onto my mother's and sister's sleeping heads.

I crawl through the tent flaps,
outside a chorus of insects and waking birds,
the ripe, pungent smell of a river that regularly
upchucks old bait cans, gutted fish and clams,
mingles with evergreen and whiffs of smoke.
Air so heavy with moisture that I lean against it
while lacing damp shoes.

Dad parts the fog with a hand that finds mine,
wispy river sprites whirl about our legs;
silhouettes and phantoms waft in and out of focus.
I spread my arms and twirl, imagine floating
through clouds with an angel at my elbow,
the world compressed, heaven accessible.
The morning holier than a cathedral.

I cannot see through the fog, but the roar of the
Muskingum chasing its own tail over the dam
grows deafening as we near the locks. We walk
the length of the slippery stone wall, jump down
and pick our way across the beach, skirt last night's
washed-up fish and mother-of-pearl shards.
We find the old outboard—just as we left her,
tethered to a concrete block above the water line.

Dad lifts me into the boat, shoves off and shimmies
over the gunwale. Rather than turn over the motor,
he defers to the river, lets loose a primal howl.
The boat slips into the current, shoots downstream

like a star mistaking indigo water for midnight sky.
Dad settles near the throttle, me at the bow watching
for turtles and kingfishers. Both of us silent, the fog and
fragile moment turning to ash beneath the sun's gaze;
my father's love palpable, solid and true as the old boat.

Sara Shearer

In the Garden

Grandpa asks
"do you know
what a butterfly's wings
feel like?"
and before I can
say no
he clamps a hand
around the monarch at rest
on the face of a flower
and it makes a crunch like cellophane
the orange
black
white
shards of it
poking out
between the fingers
of the fist he extends
to me.
His skin is dry
cracked at the wrinkles
bulging of vein.
A few fingers don't straighten out anymore
from working hard jobs he came up
Route 21 for
before they became endangered
extinct
leaving everyone
grasping at rust.
Still
he offers the shattered mess to me
insisting
"ain't it pretty?"

Robin Mullet

Garden Angel

The windowsills are cabinets of curiosity.
Stones gathered by grandchildren,
a jar of empty snake eggs, two papery skins,
feathers of every size joining dried astilbes in a vase,
a crawdad claw from the creek, a buckeye,
the skeleton of a cicada, 17 years in the forming,
a fossil of ancient coral from a sea millennia past,
and a tiny garden angel,
crow in her hat, sunflower in her arms, faded
but still keeping watch over this hodge-podge,
this wunderkammer of a forest life.

Lynette Ford

Granny Knew

Granny read the leaves, the soil, the sky, like tarot cards, like gazing glass,
read aches and sorrows like rune stones and bones.
Granny read the Bible even though she kept every word in her head,
knew which verse to breathe over a sickly child or a dying man,
knew the old ways to soothe, to heal, to sing a soul up to Glory.

Granny knew when the dry days would end,
even as the earth pleaded for salvation,
knew when storms would rage with Lord-Jesus might,
with lightning white and wild, with thunder to pound against a metal sky,
all foretold in a bloody sunrise.

Stay here in the cellar, she calmly said,
just before the neighbor's roof screamed and flew away on a spiraling wind.

Granny smelled impending death on a friend's breath.
She hugged him gently. Same day, with her dark fingers hovering
over a new bride's flat belly, she sensed a baby growing.
She foretold his sex with a rock tied to a string.
She was right. One died in a few weeks. In a few months, one was born.

Granny told me she heard an owl call three times.
That night, she died, an owl outside her bedroom window.
It rose on wings like a tempest rising,
carrying a last sweet breath to Heaven,
a last word exhaled in reconciling prayer.

Sometimes she watches now, a rust-red bird chattering
Bible verses, nodding approval
as I listen to a still-blue sky and note the leaves curling
to catch the promised rain.

Lynette Ford

Call

that call,
that lusty call,
then a blaze of red
streaking from the ruddy barberry
to the silver maple,
like a shred of burning cloth rising
against the foggy blanket of dawn

that call,
that search for one another,
that proclamation: here here here here
right here right here
then the response: right here right here
pretty pretty pretty

and the gray morning becomes beautiful,

awake, alive, passionately coupled,
life to life.

the cardinals commit to one another,
to living this new day.

I hear the call as the sky begins to burn
here right here
I am right here
this moment is pretty pretty pretty

Heidi Arnold

Grandma's Hands

I cradle Grandpa's dentures
in my left palm
brush with the right
interlock the uppers and lowers
my pointer secures the combination
snug in the blue plastic box for the night

I rake through shortening
and flour with my right fingers
hold the rim of Tupperware with my left
form pea-sized crumbs
closed hand squeezes to test
add six tablespoons of ice water

I apply soap to lenses
breathe heavy instead
wipe the glass with tissue
all fingers but the pointer
circle counterclockwise

I clasp an apple in my left three fingers
short paring knife in the right
grip and turn like a machine
pinky and ring fingers hidden beneath
cutting perfect spirals of red skins

I swing the glass door open
wind the 8-day clock
turn the key again and again
tipping the pendulum to start time

like she did

Sandra Kolankiewicz

Inheritance

There is none, something that

                      would have horrified

my grandmother, seeing

                  not just the normal wear

and tear on her possessions

                  but the kind of devolving

that can result only

                by "smoking from the

Chinaman's pipe," my

                  grandfather used to call it,

something he'd seen in

                  World War Two, never

knowing the British

                  bombed Hong Kong to make

them buy. I'd like

                to slip away too, not to see how

inappropriately my

                  sisters are dressed for the

season or be clueless

                  that no one has eaten except out

of a box for days, that

                  sweet surrendering to the

poppy that will make

                  my mother sell my body if

I'm not careful in a state

                  where cares evaporate,

wafting away in the

                  smoke from a candle or in that

bottle of pills with no

                  childproof cap she's always

shaking to make sure

                  there's some left, fingers

dipping in while she's

                  asleep, replaced with aspirin,

all her earthly

                belongings passing down to us.

Colette Tennant

What She Could Find

My great-great grandmother made necklaces
out of what she could find.
She'd boil and bleach snake skeletons and thread them
with bird bones and carved beads
into a design as satisfying as old recipes for bread.

How did it feel to wrap her throat in copperhead spines
and tiny wish bones so they rippled with each swallow?
Did she sing hymns at Gravel Hill Baptist
with sparrow bones draped over her clavicle?
Some days, did the slender remnants of water moccasin tails
tap just above her Appalachian heart?
When a lullaby quieted her babies in the night,
did something archetypal and ancient
mimic the muscles in her mother throat?

Erica Reid

This Place Does Not Care If I Am Happy

This ruby-throated world is not for me.
Not mine, this jack pine tar, this chunky sunlight.
Not mine, the eggs or weeds or garter snakes.
This limping yellow willow is not for me,
Nor is the wrinkled willow that the lake makes.

These thrushes will still be here when I go.
Maybe not this robin and maybe not these reeds
But some robin in some reeds will be here when I go.
Some or another maple, some lightning-bent bough,
Some summer-sick magnolia will be here when I go.

This place has never cared if I am happy.
The fungus does not care, the fox does not care,
The deer looked as though—for just a moment—
But no. This place does not care if I am happy.

And I am, thank you, thank you, I am.

Erica Reid

Bee, fern, worm
–For Joshua White

Adler's Bee
Apis mellifera adler

This species of Western honey bee was named for Dr. Jackson Adler, the apiologist who discovered the bee's unique hollow leg. Shortly after birth, Adler's Bee stores a bit of nutrient-rich "royal jelly" in the cavity, which then matures and ferments throughout the bee's weeks-long life. When Adler's bee senses its life is nearing its useful end, it will treat itself to the fatty jelly, its sublime sweetness acting as a sort of opiate to ease the final transition. Dr. Adler referred to his bees' savoring process as "nipping."

The Ginny Fern
Pteridophyte virginie

The Ginny fern, partial to low-light areas such as forest floors, has recently drawn some attention for a singular method of adaptation. When sensing the rare ray of sun, the fern forces water *out*, splaying small beads across the surface of its leaves through a series of fine pores. This magnifies the sunbeam and maximizes the Ginny's opportunities for photosynthesis. On a moderately bright morning, the Ginny fern can cause an entire thicket to glimmer.

"Mandala" Earthworm
Oligochaeta rex

Though visually indistinguishable from the common earthworm, the *rex*, or more commonly the "mandala" earthworm, stands out through one key mechanism: in passing soil through its system, the "mandala" leaves a bafflingly symmetrical and intricate pattern behind. The scientific community acknowledges that this worm lacks absolutely any cerebral capacity for art—the worms can scarcely process *light*, let alone logic—but one cannot help but wonder.

Ben Kline

B

Grandpa had an S for his middle name.
No period, just my S

sliding out his pink mouth like a kazoo
summoning copperhead revenants.

He fortified his sweet tea with honey, brown
pours from his flask, his theory

about mud daubers being honeybees cast
in purgatory, forced to live

in the dirt. *They never land on dandelions.*
He pointed at the yard, sunny

white florets abuzz with harvest, bumbles
and hornets bobbing trajectories.

I wanted to snatch one by the wings, ask
about their dauber cousins

whose queens order the capture of crab
and yellow spiders for the larder,

and I wanted to slice my first name
from my last with my B

like a sting when it breaks the skin.
I'm not sure how they fit

in those little pipes. Grandpa knocked one
loose from the porch corner

with his steady stick. Crumbs bounced, broke
into dust, larvae and black

eyeballs rolling into the grass, pedipalp
ghosts on the breeze.

And they're so quiet. Were I as scorned,
my sting so fraught,

I would be too.

Ben Kline

Let Us Pray

Our pile of cousins congregates at 8:30, stacks hickory and elm atop old
Tribunes, oak leaves gasping for the match.

The first cousins bring beer and joints, plastic jugs of sour water to numb
our tongues.

Above the pit and switchgrass, embers crack darkness. Coals stay up all night.

Pop, pretzels and chips, sleeping bags arrive with the second cousins.

                                                    Ursa Major watches.

The thirds craft cover stories about the drive-in, collect cash for next time.

                                        Every cousin brings their pocketknife.

I open mine
last, cleanse
the blade with spit
and flame. It glows,
a stick of sunset

cooling pink as inside
my lips. In the pile
I split my ring finger's tip,
blood hissing between tongues
and smoke. The cut

flares. Did you know, a third asks,
fire is a chemical reaction outside of any state of matter?
                                                              Yes, I do,

                        wavering between starlight and our ash.

Donna Hilbert

Mother Tongue
–for my grandmother, Appalachian born and raised

My mother tongue
unrolls along the red dirt plain:
slow, tacky,
unfolding like the dream
that catches everything.

My red mother tongue
unrolls in rows of cotton,
alfalfa, fields of wheat,
and in the green water
of the silty river.

And in the back yard
on a summer's night, in grass
thick with chiggers,
red ants, stickers.
My slick mother tongue

switches legs for talking ugly,
pitching a fit, throwing a hissy.
My slick red sticky mother tongue
can lick any little pistol,
and keeps the ring-tailed tooters

toeing the line.

Jacob Phillis

To Drink the Day's Last Bottle

The morning sun rises in the east,
With the fresh leaves of Autumn awakening,
The residents of Salt Run rise up for new feats.
One of these individuals was William,
A worker in a small town, in a small valley.
Yet, his entire life felt as if it lacked enthusiasm.

A father figure to many, William was,
Where he teaches his children in an open field.
The subjects included literature and math in class,
The days roll past, hour by hour,
As generations of youth turn old.
Then, the night falls in with whisky sour.

All coins have their rusty side,
Similarly, William isn't any different.
His work would begin at moon's time,
And by morning, he would have a ha'penny.
Perhaps it would buy a piece of candy,
Or he would've been drunk-a-plenty.

The afternoon sun sets in the west,
With the creek water slowly rippling through.
The residents of Salt Run fall into deep rest,
William, however, would have his last drink,
That night, he dreams of a bird.
The bird leaving its brink,
Never to turn back.

Margo Taft Stever

Beulah Reid

The switches line up
by your bed, wolves' teeth,
and you, cruel nanny,
use them in your finest dreams.
Your nose mounts a grand plot
to take over your face
each time you show us
the noise birches make.
The sticks we find outside,
you turn against us.
Some are blunt, others sharp,
spring-loaded. You twist them before us.

Rustling and rumbling
through underbrush with packs
of dogs, we smell of rotting
leaves, everything going back, the rough
welter blending into earth.
One night you crack the window.
You hiss with damnation
even a preacher couldn't better—
"You kids ain't nothin' but a bunch of hillbillies."

Night after night I witness
your red vinyl rocking chair,
your stockings pulled down over ankles,
the corridors of your white bulging
legs, your jutting veins, while bubbles
float over *The Lawrence Welk Show,*
and Liberace pounds his piano
with dumb passion.

Hattie Sells Clarke

Planting the Riverbank

Like insects ourselves we crawl the slope
armed with trowels and hand rakes
and plastic pots.
Punch holes through sun battered plastic
and plant, and plant,
and plant.
All morning.
Spiderwort, milkweed and buttonbush,
wingstem and blue aster.

We kneel, kowtow, prostrate ourselves
with backs and knees that mutter disapproval.
Dirt in the worn-through fingers of gloves
dirt insinuating itself into sneakers
the taste of dirt.

Along the road above us
scurry of earliest fallen leaves.
Beside us
buzzing of our creature clients
waved away (with apologies).
Behind us the river
hauling down the sky's disposition
and nudging it along an ancient path.

Finally, we stand back to survey.

We are looking at still bare stretches of mulch
Pale, flowerless stalks
frail and stubborn as old women.
We are looking at small green spaces salted with our own sweat.

But we are seeing July.

Diana Becket

Work let him go

but he stays to watch
the winter sunshine link
tree shadows
along the creek banks,
the cabin walls catch
glimmers stark
against the meadow's
shade. Beams twist twigs
in his mind into traceries
of silver against a blue sky
that mocks him. Light
refracts tree reflections,
deepens branch and trunk
curves until they glow
in underwater worlds
of connection—
no longer a part
of his life.

He can't pay the rent
after tomorrow
but this evening,
he traces the sun-rays
until they sink
behind a ridge
of hills and glint
on gliding night hunters'
wing feathers
channeling air currents
down over slopes
to the river. Orange fire
ripples the waves
until the final flames
outline the horizon's hills
and twilight is pulled
into night.

Nancy Susanna Breen

How Lilly Applegate Helped
Uncle Jim Save the Family

Grandma loved to say
none of us would be here
if Grandpa's Uncle Jim
hadn't stood up to Dr. Forman.
Two of the boys had been fighting,
and Great-Grandma, great
with child, got into the middle
of the brawl, was pushed
backwards out of a window,
and went into labor.

When the doctor examined her,
he said, "Oh, the baby's breech.
I'm going to have to cut
the baby in two to save the mother."
Uncle Jim said, "No baby gets cut in two
in my house." So Great-Grandma
delivered Grandpa somehow,
although no one ever gave details
about that part of the story.

No one ever said whether she had
a C-section or how much she suffered.
No one ever said, "Wow,
that Lilly Applegate, she brought
that baby safely into the world."
It was Uncle Jim who got to be the hero,
while Great-Grandma was relegated
to the shadowy background,
absorbed in the typical woman's work
of breaking up fights and pushing out sons.

C.F. Kinney

The Pain and the Body that Belong to Us

It comes on so gradually, you're not even sure you notice it.
And then when you do

when the suffering signals to you as
a million desperate ships
sinking in the ocean of your own spinal fluid
flashing panic
into the void
of your
determination to withstand the forces of humanity and nature
stoic and in bad company

when the suffering signals that
this is all
too
much, you redouble your efforts

as though maybe if you try hard enough
you can will your own body out of existence.

Just step right out of it like dropping
a hotel bathrobe on the floor, a
temporary luxury
that never belonged to you anyway.

Are we not
only temporary
in this flesh with
these fingerprints?
Why try to guard these arms that love the evening air?

So instead of marveling at your own
knees that bend
to bring you to a cat's solemn countenance

you work harder
and you ignore it.
You stand in the lighthouse and close your stone eyelids.
You forget what life is outside this pain,
begin to imagine agony
has some inherent virtue.

And then you forget your own thoughts
and have to borrow someone else's

but they don't fit quite right
so only leave you miserable
and adrift.

Until one day
your elbows lead a mutiny, force the realization that

if you refuse to make the acquaintance of your own sinew
if you can't learn the rivers of your own feet

if you will this body
this world
this water
to nothing

you will have nowhere
left to go.

Becca J.R. Lachman

Choreography Of The Barren

There are only certain days   you'll have the energy to send
the Valentine   like the photo   reply to the shower invite
do a loving kindness meditation   scatter wildflower
seeds   mail the birthday package   put on the holy
armor   call your doctor about new meds, options, test
results   give back the heirloom ring passed from daughter
to daughter   throw out the musty collection of letters
answer the RSVP   send a welcome baby basket

open the Christmas card   open the Christmas
card   open   text "Gah! I'm so excited for you!"   sit
with no book in the lunchroom   think of every 1 in 10 women
at a dance recital/concert/basketball game (you aren't alone, along
in a crowd)

take it out on the dinner vegetables   hold yourself up
on the way up the staircase   avoid mirrors for a day or two
stuff dried dates with almond butter, dunk in simmering chocolate
eat about a dozen   stand outside and watch the weather
jump 30 degrees in a number of hours   brace yourself against
the wind of it   wake up thinking about all the women
who couldn't or shouldn't, and did   forgive them   forgive
yourself (how many ways can you say this?)   and thank
your body, anyway, over a warm cup of tea, its soft
wet breath

Wendy McVicker

At night, she plays with shadows

Her hands form birds
and butterflies, dogs

silently barking.
Snow drifts and settles

on the roof outside
her window, blue

glass gleams on the sill.
She watches her dreams

sift past, the world
unaccountably changed, dressed

in another topography.
Once, the mountains called her,

their dazzling verticality.
She left them

for these low green hills,
woods where nothing

echoes, nothing
rings out sharply

against the walls
of the world.

The soft earth sinks
beneath her feet.

She listens carefully,
the air is thick with buzzing.

She can't make out the voices
that call her name

Wendy McVicker

also known as surprise lilies

The resurrection lilies
have risen, more numerous

than ever, a flock
of pink birds hovering

over the weeds
and exhausted
August grass.

After the bike wreck—
cracked ribs and shattered
spleen—

they were pink trumpets
saluting my return
to life, waving me

into the light
after all that darkness.

This second summer
of the pandemic,
they almost take flight.

Fluty and pink,
they shimmer
in the shadows, hum

in the sorrow
at the heart
of this storm.

Susan Grimm

Some Like It Blog

Lilacs of the past still grow in your yards and beards,
I've heard, are the new regime. Each man a prophet

with his chin-lap of hair. Walt Whitman, I am not
on that train. But these lilacs with their purple sweet

message in the corner by the garage showing up
on Google Earth. Maybe a hundred years of digging

in like a burr where there was once a hardwood forest.
The theater with its evening veil of bats has been torn down,

but you can still hear church bells at noon. Cement
replaces slate, a parade ground of trees torn from

their sewer roots. But still dandelions wheedle, rabbits
burgeon. Dirt remains diggable. Rain falls (some).

Peggy Rowan

Family Reunion

I am scared of these hills,
the memories,

scared of getting sucked up
in nostalgia,

air thick, trails narrow,
the past—

faded shadows
in the dying sun.

Cathy Cultice Lentes

The Wild

He's come to this place for years, first as a boy
learning manhood, the killing of what's best to eat, the
killing of what's deemed pest. His people run deep here.

With pride he tells of the Bible, curling with unreadable
script, scooped from the mud by his second great granny
as Confederate Morgan and his Raiders roared through.

His father gone two years, he returns to the woods he loves,
remembering dank days on foot following deer trails up, up
and over hills dense with sumac, towering sycamore, and

maple. The hard quiet of waiting, still as a rabbit, hunkered
low like leaf debris on the forest floor, or perched high as a crow
in a bare-limbed tree, still and serious, waiting for buck or doe

to break cover. Gun poised, tension rising in his gut,
shoulders hard, hands steady: patience, patience,
pop, and recoil.

These days, he and his brothers, and their sons mount
four-wheelers before dawn, motor to tree stands or hunker
with heat packs in a blind, sipping coffee from a Yeti jug.

The deer follow old trails, rely on familiar scent and sound,
flash the same white flags as their ancestors, hiding when
the world says *be still*, the wild ripe with bobcat spray,

coyote scat, the musk and babel of men.

Michael Henson

That's it

That whisper of sand in the wind
that secret in the frozen stone
that web of frost in the grass
that crown of sun-tipped branches in the sycamore.

That's it!
That's what I wanted to tell you!

Keri Johnson

Ridgetops

Borne out of foothills,
      I walked the fertile earth.
      I saw blue herons and crawdads
      in flooded fields and emerald waters of winding creeks.
      I saw white puffs of untamed morning glories
      dancing in lush roadsides.
      I saw the delicate fawn and mother doe
      Fearful and inquisitive, posed in a winsome wheat field.

And I saw hilltops—naked, exploited, stripped—and homes in neglect.
      I saw men who thought they were important,
      But not important enough.
      I saw women who gave all their love,
      For nothing in return.
      I saw children who ran gleeful and free,
      Blissfully hungry, rambunctious, and naive.

And then I journeyed back home;
      Climbed out of the hollows and raced onto the ridgetop.
      Where I stood tall and faced a feral sunrise,
      Whispering a prayer,
      Kissing everything it touched.

Richard Westheimer

Uncommon ground

I.
Bobby pulled back the tarp, revealed
the bloodless head, the rack intact
of the buck he felled with one clean shot.
For thirty days of autumn dawns, he'd sat
strapped to the stand, high up in the old sycamore,
his back to the creek his eyes on the edge
where the scrub wood becomes field. With his hands,
which were numbed with the waiting, he held
a longbow nocked, ready to loose a shaft
into the darkest part of the twelve pointer
he'd spied for weeks from too far away,
until today.

II.
Once, at dusk, not long ago, Bobby missed the heart
of what must have been the king of our small wood,
a mighty one who did not drop when shot,
who bolted through the undergrowth, arrow shafting
from his side, vanished as if an apparition
in the falling night, dripped a trail of liquid rubies,
spots of blood on fallen leaves. Bobby scrambled from his stand,
tracked the tortured prey, longed to make his kill complete,
to relieve the creature of its suffering. But, right at last light
rain began to fall, washed away the red stains, rendered
the trail mute. Bobby wept the tears of Tantalus,
blundered into the dark, heaved hopeless breaths
much like the stumbling buck.

III.
Bobby showed me his new hardware, a camo-clad night scope
slotted atop his AR. He ran his hand from barrel to stock,
eyed the sight, said to me, *I'll try to take out that coyote
tonight, the one that stared you down the other day.*
I am grateful, though I know—this man who loves the sun rising
over our creek, stills his breath to match the windless dawns,

hears the morning whisper "amen"—this man
who hauls in his saw to take out dead falls, helps
whenever he can, calls our place Eden—yes, this man
of Saxon build, flies the yellow flag—on it a coiled snake
that hisses *don't you tread on me*—so, I am afraid
that late at night, he is sure the news is fake, believes
there are elites out to replace his kind, maybe
suspects I am one of those he's wary of.

Brooklyn Lengyel

Quiet Song

Today the cardinals sing quietly
Coyotes howl their mournful song

A chorus echoed in every yard
And from the ponds the frogs croak a refrain

That the flies return with a lonely melody
But the cardinals sing quietly

Their song an ode of joy
A spot of red against the white snow

Their song swallowed by noises of life
Clawed feet clutched onto decaying branches

Music alive in each gnarled trunk
In every coop and barn

In the quiet hum of every home
As the winter brings a silence so thick

That for a moment bears a clarity
Wherein the subtle crescendo becomes a symphony

Leslie Clark

Interior

Drawn-out
summer evenings.
Rind of moon.
Leaves on the
trees are denser,
more privacy
for the birds.

In the maple,
a dusk-red
cardinal twines
in and around.
Quiet, purposeful.

In the spaces
between leaves,
a hint of color
flashes, is gone,
reappears,
pulsing in and out
of the green—
the beating heart
of the living wood.

Mark Jordan

The Watchers

The stag stood on the hill,
silhouetted against the sky.
In the moonless night I walked,
reeling from another loss,
but brought up short
by the thicker blackness
drawn together above me.
I froze, the stag's neck arched,
his antlers poking holes
in the cloud shelf
pulling across the stars.

I knew the promontory
where he stood, the place
draped with a blanket,
a glint of ancient energy,
the place where the spirits,
the watchers of the world,
overlooked the unfurling
of this glacial valley,
the last furrow the ice cut
before running aground
against Appalachia.
Many nights I've felt them,
lined in static processional
along the gravelly low ridge
risen up from the valley floor
like the spine of a sleeping panther,
who waits to be called some distant day
to battle the thunderbird. I could feel
their gravity, their dizzy giddiness,
their position outside of time,
like a gibbous eye poking
through the membrane,
velvet skin of space,
to watch us dance.

For still ages,
the stag and I stood.
Another deer blasted a snort
from the cemetery atop the hill,
and the stag answered. Then I did, too.
Behind the cemetery sycamores, I could see
Orion, not yet covered by the clouds of forgetfulness,
glittering, glittering like he had a right to shine
despite the hadal trench of loss I brought,
a shadow I dragged through the dark.
The other deer drew back, but
the stag stayed, for
minutes or
ages.

Finally,
I unwound,
letting the tension
spin off my limbs and drop,
until nothing but stories flowed
between us. The stag spoke to me,
told me that he was a watcher,
had stood on that hill since
the ice made a new face
of this living land,
but beyond too,
not living
in our clocks
nor looking
out our windows.
From here, he watches
the slow turn of the sky
as the world's mind
finds its hands,
its instruments,
its words,
itself.

He invited me
to take my place
on the spine of the hill.

As I walked up, the buck
galloped along the track as if
we were to converge at the top,
before the boneyard gate, but then
disappeared over the ridge's brow
and was nowhere to be found
by the time I reached top.
Instead, Orion stood
glimmering, his limbs
outlined in starstuff dust.
For many years, I was drawn
to that sketch of stars, half expecting
the hunter to turn some cold winter night
and shoot his blazing arrows directly at me.
But standing on the cairn of dreams pooled atop
that ancient glacial radiant, suddenly I understood
for the first time that Orion would not turn to shoot me,
because Orion was not a hunter at all, and his arc was no bow.

What that star man reaches for is his harp, sacred and quivering
a different kind of arrow, the piercing shaft of arcing voice.
I raised my arms in wonder, then turned around to see
a vast triangle of mackerel sky, another harp,
carved by the antlers of the stag,
each string of clouds chiming
the notes of silver stars
brushing as they
drew past.

Turning back to Orion,
I watched a shooting star pass
through his harp and into his groin core.
My sorrow hummed as grace. At once I saw that every loss,
every friend who slips this crude vale with unfinished heart-music,
becomes a plangent string on my own harp, a story to sing,
a bloodflower bloom that launches the glow of dawn
spreading over these wrinkled leathery hills,
a blaze of chemistry finding a spiral,
on its way to pry open
a million eyes.

Barry Yeoman

Winter Morning

Crows scavenge
last night's roadkill.

Small animals traverse
steaming ditches.

The breath of cows
hovers over icy tufts.

Already, contrails
crisscross the sky.

Driving to the factory,
I spill my hot coffee

and scald myself.
All my huge dreams

hibernate now.
I once believed

death was slow.

Barbara Lyghtel Rohrer

Cooper's Hawk

There he was perched
on my deck as I stepped
into the kitchen
early that morning.

I froze
not wanting my movement
to scare him away.

He flew.

Would he return?

Early the next morning
I jumped up to see—*no.*

But when I lay back down
to doze a bit more,
I heard wings beating
behind me.

Not his,
my own.

Mitchell James

Deer Stand

I study the deer stand
and how the morning frost
clings to it
23 degrees now
soon to be 50
though it be February

It makes me think of that 12-point buck
that "just escaped" you
and how you lost your Maxima Red
in the haunches of that lie
drinking that night
hollering at the walls
about how the arrow
set you back a bill

You know
I found that arrow
angled in the foliage
the following spring
and the bottles
and Sterilite tub of blankets
in that old gristmill
you always scared me away from
said it would collapse into the creek
that the water wheel
would grind me to Cream of Wheat

Every time you'd laugh
like it was the first time you'd said it
and I'd eat my Cream of Wheat
and think about consuming myself
until the dish was clean
but for those stubborn bits that cling
like sand
to the belly

of the bowl
The tree stand
it will not last long
It already sags
as if you're in it

Mom is moving on
There's no new man
but the music in the house
is different now
and the smells of dinner
and how she holds her wine glass
when she laughs

Your bottles of liquor
have not stirred
They just make caramel prisms of light
gather the detritus of day
and shoulder it
into night

You must look closely
at the bottles to see
how much covers them
for they do not lean
below the gravity of life
like the deer stand
which will fall
before the tree that holds it.

David B. Prather

Crows Or Ravens

No one here seems to know the difference, or even care.
All that can be said is that crows are clever,
          always clever.
They teach their fledglings how to recognize
what can harm and what can kill.

All we know of ravens is just as much—
how close one feather lies next to another.
How difficult it is to see
the difference between unkindness and murder,
impossible to know the subtleties
between storytelling and conspiracy.

I might correct my friends by suggesting
treachery is larger, reminding them
scarecrows are people without souls.

And birds revel with souls, guide us to a flimsy hereafter,
keep us safe on the road from here to where,
          from this to there.

No one here seems to know rook or jackdaw,
          midnight or sable.
But sometimes all we have left is forgiveness, a chance
to understand so little of this world is observed,
even as we look to the heavens,
the silhouettes of flight indistinguishable, all of us
          taking our turns in the sky.

David B. Prather

Why I Cannot Leave

Late summer humidity languishes
mold upon my sleep. By morning,

the aroma of death pushes up
through soil from roots of trees

long fallen. This fungus is the wisdom of earth,
twists and folds of some dark intellect

escaping flesh that always rots and falls
away. To where I cannot say.

These are the wraiths of maples,
vestiges of twenty-five years or more,

hollow trunks, peeling bark, bare branches,
heartwood reduced to dust.

My heart is here with sorrel and self-heal,
with knotweed and floss flower.

These are the words of home,
syllables slipping easily off the tongue.

I would hold you here on the banks of the Ohio
where every chemical leaches into roots

of sycamore and willow,
but there is hell

beneath us, beneath every street,
beneath every sidewalk, beneath every bridge,

beneath every building where we stand
and sit and lie. I will not lie.

Within a day or two, reclamation begins,
saprophytes withdrawn.

And I am left to wonder which ghosts are next,
who will visit, who will leave me

here at the end of a season
with no reason to pray. With no reason to move on.

Julie L. Moore

The Jersey Girl Adjusts to Rural Living

Our neighbors own a rooster named Rocky.
It crows all day long, as though it doesn't understand
its calling. My daughter says she likes the whines
rising from its throat. They make her feel at home.

While the cock struts like a bad & brash boy,
my dog is blasé, barely caring. No surveillance in the yard.
No bark, no howl. It's my other daughter who
growls about the noise. Think of Jesus, my mother tells her,

let Rocky bring to mind lessons about betrayal
& remorse. At sunrise, when I take out the dog,
the chickens stir, & I mistake their sound
for babies whimpering the way they do

when they first awake, when hunger
stings their bellies, just before they cry.
Out of the Ohio blue emerging above,
a primitive tingle begins to slink up my spine.

Clarissa Jakobsons

Hostel Spaces at Malabar Farm

Swallow poems, churn words
beyond the hill of trees. Curled leaves
tremble from heaven's embrace.

The painter's brush freezes each moment.
Two-firm crosses anchor an empty laundry line
while a stiff American flag wavers on Malabar Farm.

Stacked wooden logs brace each other,
as diesel fumes trail roadside and geese holler
across the pond. Ducks and sparrows

answer free-range questions. Cobwebs
fill a watering can next to a shovel
                              and resting broom.

Scattered stars and poets are planted on earth
with hungry pangs while chickadees peck,
and squawks surround the empty swing—

Ceely's ghost glides back and forth, her hand
extends throughout the day. Silent pens rush
beyond the fire pit. Lavender touches matrix

glow, I kiss pink thyme, hopley's
oregano against chipped white paint
with Kentucky spearmint.

Brittle leaves dust a baby's cry.
Sage wind-gods dust Malabar Farm.
Come sit with us, Ceely Rose.

Clarissa Jakobsons

Moonlight
–Martins Ferry, honoring James Wright

The orb of night wanes
embracing coolness as poplar
leaves tumble through air to ground
in broken thoughts.

Gather Gala
apples for winter's hearth
before our year passes—
Embrace sunlight's energy.

Dance naked
under the moon's umbrella,
shift thoughts, bake bread.
Forgive what ails.

Elaine Costanzo

Ohio Summers

In that small town we
made summer friends, knew
their names like long-lost cousins
waiting to be found. Transported
ourselves Virginia to Ohio
on childhood's gossamer filament.
It stretched on forever. Learned life
in the safety of small-town darkness,
played "doctor" behind garages set
on alleys—odd little gravel roads laid
with black, sticky tar by midsummer
to harness dust that coated windows,
misted July flower beds. Bare feet were
dark, with rocky feel between our toes.
What didn't pass in front, passed in back.
The cakewalk at Homecoming,
and boys with strange Midwest accents
growing up just like you. Made you feel
exotic in such a simple place, but was
only the sound of cornfields and tractor's
hum meshed into an earthiness
of budding awareness. Overalls
were romantic. Manure was sweet to smell.
Ohio summers, gone forever,
fresh sliced peaches in a milk glass bowl.
Only red stains left swimming
in residue of white milk. The silver spoon
touches bottom.

Ed Davis

Ephemera

Stalking snow trillium, we climb up the bluffs,
stopping to scrutinize these three-pronged stars
contained in tiny dirt pockets in mossy, sun-splashed
rock so easily lost to casual hikers' gaze.
"They live for a day, maybe two," our guide says.
All that energy that took four years to store before
white blooms burst into rock garden bouquets.

On up Cedar Run Trail, through hepatica, blue on white;
salt and pepper, scouring rush and harbinger of spring,
all to be gone in a matter of only a few days.
"Notice the hickory's complex interweaving bark, made
to protect itself from the elephants roaming Ohio
all those millennia ago." She smiles at our skepticism.

And further up to the place clear-cut in recent years,
now populated by saplings and dead red cedars.
"Horses did it. First old growth was cut for farming;
when soil played out, it became meadow for grazing horses;
then the cedars grew until tractors replaced the horse.
Back grew the hardwoods, shadowing the cedars."

She cuts a branch, holds it to her nose and sighs,
delivers it into my palm. Bone-white outside,
the heartwood inside is dried blood-red,
and what's dead still lives in scent and sight.

Kenneth Armitage Kawaji

The Road to Goshen

Hope resided here once. Farmed
out of a frame bent house
loaned out burned sight
down on Eight Ball road
low under Goshen on the Pike
now the old 2 lane blacktop
covered in sticky mulberries
tire mashed seeds mingled hop
with a hundred buckeyes
shot out of as many heads
lolling upward gaze
dead reckons
meth dead dogs
beasts, and burdens
as black swollen as the crows
crown floating in the spiral
of a dust devil stows
wing out above and below
brethren caw, haw, hee and angle
all aerodynamics and unceasing hunger
for bright objects tangled and seeds.
The neighbors corn and pole beans
the white church under a darkening
thunderhead toward fifty feet of gutters
pitched creek ward and away
from the foundations mud
clay, and topsoil and lightning torn
fires the shoulders of the hills
bent over hat and the ridge of the brow
eyes cleared the acres
of oak and distant dreams
of moon calves, how
in the kudzu, the oak leaves
and sumac ivy, goats
in the scree
feeding in the mist.

212

Push back the hat, he nods
bent low in the rain weight
his hard hands furrows wet
the dream-streaked scar. The ghost
needle tracked colored
angel dust cloud powdered
red neck
wrangles the rain drover
reads the signs; the tracks filled in
the storm gullies running, dead
junked parked cars
off the hill round pastures, the lime
stone dinted blade, the hedge
sparrows bunked song bush
first light robins sing, the cock start
crow cries the never-ending sound.
The pecker wood heart
what god makes stay the heat beats
the light from the day
a fierce hardened promise
the man-made drawn
in a bowl of clay.

Jackie Kalbli

Corn

Aunt Violet's truck careened
on a curve out of Sandy Hook
toward Isonville and
dumped her with a load
of coal into a ravine,
leaving her mind wrong.

She lived with her mommy after that,
in the house on stilts.

The two vanilla-scented old ladies
matched like a sweater twin-set.
Us kids couldn't tell them apart
and called them both Granny.

They were tall and boney,
wore long dresses,
rolled their corn silk hair
into tight muffin buns at the neck,
and smoked cob pipes.

They kept a free-range cow,
tossed dried corn to the chickens
that scratched under the house,
and lived like benign trolls
beside a crick.

The laying out of Granny Alice
was a featherbed
as warm as a kitten,
was a feast of puffy white cake
on a corn-flowered plate.

Randi Ward

Dog Days

Gnats
wriggle
towards
sunburned
temples;
I just shuck
another
ear
and yawn.

S. Renay Sanders

You Youngins' Be Careful Around That Well

The ancestors placed
The rainbow over the mountain
Welcoming generations
Back to the valley, back home

Asphalt smooth against the tires
But in my bones, I felt the rumble of
Dirt road beneath me, long time gone
The child within knew she was near the journey's end

Once again, walking time-space
Where little girls imagined
Porch post boyfriends, practicing splintered kisses
Across that creek bed, we cousins played house

In the gentle mist of the cove
Then and now
The spirits of home
Descend upon my soul

From pillar to post
Running the fence line
Trumpet flowers blasting
Announcing the travelers' arrival

Fragrance of honeysuckle
With each breath taken
A cloud of red dust
Fogging the dirt road

Mimosas drape
The stone-walled well
Swaying in the barely breeze
Bucket at the ready

Awakening the blooms of memories
Story told of the grandfather then Daddy
Rescuing his son from the waters deep
Courage gathered

On tiptoe
I leaned over, peering down
Bucket dropped
Retrieving a dippered sip

Kerry Trautman

The Remains of Eden

–Rev. Edmund Landon West, in 1908, proposed
that Great Serpent Mound in Adams County, Ohio
was the literal site of the biblical Garden of Eden.

Yes, I could be tempted here,
Reverend.
I could be convinced to eat
only native fruits,
to spit
the seeds back to
the earth,
and tend to what sprouts there
thoroughly as I tend to
what births from my hips,
what winds its way
in from
tiny serpent-like cells in
my deep darkness,
what wriggles its way
out again
to swallow what fruits of mine
I offer its mouth.

Yes, I can see how someone
and I
might be coaxed into
lying in the sculpted green
of this cliffside,
amongst all the trees of Paradise,
the warm strength
of Earth's centuries below,
ceaseless wavering of stars above,
and, in between,
four Rivers
joined and rushing
like my own blood,
ultimately outward.

Kerry Trautman

Rock House
–Hocking Hills State Park, Logan, Ohio

My daughters climb, the older girl's arm
extended, hovering behind the younger's
lower back in case of stumbling.

They disappear into the Rock House's
sweeping yawn, condensation trickling
down sandstone—never finishing its
epochs-long wet erosion.

They trail fingertips on stone walls
in which Adena women once baked bread.
Their rubber soles step over dips
where Delaware burnt log sap to turpentine.

Daylong we've hiked through winding
mossy corridors and wooded trails
criss-crossed in tree roots like boot laces

down down cliffsides terraced barely
deep enough for footholds, too focused on
center of gravity to look up and spot
the birds whose voices call out.

The girls are shadowed in echoes of
earthen womb, where once thieves and
bootleggers hid, curled against cold stone.

Imagine how easily an arrowed army or
SWAT team could swarm down
from rock ledges above, cornering those who
shiver here in this pit of earth.

If the girls called to me from the echoes,
would I be able to discern their voices
from all the others?

R McNiece

The Callings

Sundays came a light that baptized
the warped, whitewashed boards of the Layman Methodist Church.
Inside it swirled along brown-yellow grain of benches
polished smooth by generation upon generation of backsides.
What stayed mundane was the sermon, big words
children had no need to understand
to enter the heaven of the sun.
How long-winded he was, *GAWED*,
boring, boring, boring rote out of the preacher's mouth
till you wanted him to swallow a fly—
I pinched my arm to stay awake.

But when the choir rose in their white blouses,
their singing whelmed through my lungs
like light through the tall blue golden stained windows,
I followed not the verses of the hymn,
but the hum of our voices as they flowed
out the oaken doors, over the rolling hills,
down the hollow and flashed across the creek
as dozens of dragonfly wings.

After the service, the women in their floral
polyester dresses, gossiped in knots
and old men uncomfortable in starched collars
gathered around beat-up pick-up trucks
splattered with the same red clay they came from,
spit long strings of tobacco juice and talked low
down in a way I leaned towards.

I edged away from the candied condescension
of the preacher and found my body released
to the field suddenly golden, all hallelujah
breaking loose as I ran and ran, and stood whirling still
surrounded by trees full of cicadas
rasping their seventeen year prayers
stoked by gusts of solar flares

that blessed also my face.
Falling to earth then,
I laid there below the head tall hay
a long while listening
to the sheer cartilage of grasshoppers clattering
aloft from stem to stem, to the dipsy doodles songs
that startled a mockingbird's throat
as if for the first time, to the green river unraveling
through the fat-leaved shade maples,
fat upturned leaves breezing hosannas on high,
and closer, to the crickets burrowed under the dark soil
scraping the husks of their bodies wholly
into music—all those callings
I follow now, into that other world
from which this world grows,
into singing light.

Though we've been here
Ten Thousand years,
Bright shining as the sun,
We've no less days
To sing God's praise
Then when we first begun.

R McNiece

Tomatoes

Ohio river valley summer hummed wavering heat,
setting sun copper cowbell ringing distance
brought home by drop of salty sweat on lip.

Tomatoes big as a baby's bawling head
plump as a thunderstorm
hefted straight from Grandma's garden,
fat slices fanned on white porcelain platter
sprinkled with rock salt and pepper,

served every evening meal
as cicadas churred diminuendo,
scent of cherrywood wafting
from unfolded dining table,

hearts of slimy green seeds like frog spawn,
bull frog croaking dusk from the pond
down yonder, din of crickets coming on—
that juice pungent.

Cousin Glenna and her girlfriends,
teen terry cloth shorts and halter tops,
giggling along the horse fence line field backyard

singing Sinatra's strangers in the night/
exchanging glances
with hillbilly twangs,
out back beyond the garden

amid the lightening bugs they sing,
with all those hard green tomatoes still unpicked
and filling with heavy dark heat that made them
so ripe, so salty sweet.

Mark Kuhar

the silos, red-sided, silver-topped

when the leaves fall off the trees
you begin to see the silos,

red-sided, silver-topped,

stark, standing on the edge of the field,

birds in orbit
around planetarium domes,

absence
of any barn, it's just the tall silos

maybe a half-wall of quarried
limestone blocks, the foundation
of something long since gone

that which you can see in the
gnawing daylight,

is all that is there

Rose Smith

Backspin

Thrill ride at no cost, you could have called it:
The last great approach of the ride
home from church on January Sundays when
fresh inches snowed the ice on our back hill.

We knew getting up demanded more already
than last night's salt, tire chains, whispered prayers
to muscle Granddad's Oldsmobile 88 up
that 40-degree grade with all of us in tow.

How much more precarious the times we'd see
neighborhood boys had braved the angle
sledded away a full night's preparation,
left icy gleam enough to make a deacon swear.

If street across the bend was clear enough, he took
a running start up Margaret to grab the one sweet spot,
that slight bump in the angle inches high
that melted first if we were blessed with sun.

Sometimes even that start could make an old Olds
dance, become a siren, its lavender hips swaying
to the maker's tune, its owner's grip the only sign
we'd almost skidded back to Wellington or hell.

Traffic never stopped enough to notice our hill,
collisions waiting broadside for a blink, a swerve
a stall down at street level while the boys watched,
sleds in hand, to get back to their morning worship.

Sometimes he'd brake to let us out, tell us to go get sand.
or sometimes salt, always an excuse for us to leave
danger riding back-seat with him, that impending clash
with someone's lack of caution unless the grace of God.

David Garrison

Folding Tables and Five Card Stud

Gospel hour on the radio
and my grandmother joined in
Yes, we'll gather at the river,
the beautiful, the beautiful river . . .
Then she told me about Sunday mornings
when the congregation was haunted
by that cry from the pulpit,
"Where will *you* spend eternity?"
About camp meetings
where they barked Satan up a tree
and people who got saved or healed
would tremble for days on end;
about river baptisms
with the preacher holding one arm
and a deacon the other
because the current was so swift
that converts had been known
to slip from reach and drown.

She joked that Baptists
never make love standing up
because it's too much like dancing,
and she confided that Brother Felthouse
always called a *card table*
a *folding table*
because he didn't want his flock
getting any ideas.
Sometimes, before Granny dealt
the first hand of the evening,
she would ask the whole family to
Please rise and sing
our invitation hymn,
"*Just As I Am.*"
After the first few lines,
the only ones we knew,
she would say, "Amen, brothers and sisters!
Now ante up, the game is five card stud!

David Garrison

The End is Near

Jesus is everywhere
on the highway,
his rusty blue cross
placed between two yellow ones
or wreathed in plastic flowers,
draped in banners bearing names.
The skeletal remains
of a giant bust of the Savior,
destroyed a few months back
by lightning, teeter in the wind.

Trust Jesus in black spray paint
and *Jesus Saves*
in white block letters
above the throb of traffic.
Radio preachers spread fear
of the Lord far and wide.
Suddenly, red taillights
flash ahead of me.
I slam on the brakes
and whisper His name.

Jeremy Jusek

Return to Earth

Ahead of work-roughened municipal trucks
unloading dirt and gravel along Cherokee Orchard Road,
beyond the flapjack huts, themed mini golf resorts
and green mowed grass each an oasis
            among trees and concrete

Beyond straight roads and Dollywood, aging schools
gas stations, bars, and signs—oh the signs!—for
advertisers. Signs of activities. Signs of evenings
            giving way to morning, beyond the bustle

and up Le Conte, beyond the falls where
the tourists slow from a stream to a trickle,
up the steadily sharpening slope, slick scarps
stretching in both directions, the path
            increasingly less a suggestion over time

In February, the air cold and thin, where
Bullhead Trail meets Rainbow Falls,
            that is where I died for the first time

That is where I returned to Earth, close
to a mile above sea level. The squirrels waved,
glad you could finally join us they say,
prancing around red spruce blanketed in snow
            I could hear the silence

and taste the undercurrents of the soil
as sure as dipping my hand in the stream.
there my death had no meaning, stretching up
and over the cabins on Le Conte's peak
and down the other side over the Alum Bluffs,
dissipating
            among its coyotes and hibernating bears

and when I was brought to, stitched together
with the care and grace of a blind valley fae,

the grease-dipped vines holding my innards in
and the fireflies in my ribcage fascinating
but devilishly ticklish, I head home
        and learn self-control in traffic

Denton Loving

Do You Hear the Cicadas?

And how about the whippoorwill?
I hear him late into night, nearly
four decades gone from these
wooded foothills but returned
to sound his warrior song
whip-poor-weel, whip-poor-weel—
turf warning as well as mating call—
a blast that rips through my sleep
some nights and leaves me to lie
awake and wonder about choices
I've made. And I wonder why
the whippoorwill was so long silent—
probably too much pesticide,
not enough moths and beetles,
all the too usual reasons.
What makes him think things
will be different this time? What
calls him back? What sustains
this small nightjar's blind bravery?

Denton Loving

Girl in the Woods

Before the earth became her bed, she raked away
　　　the rubble and rocks, scraped the soil smooth.

There are no candy men here, no dope peddlers,
　　　no pill pushers, no one to hand out 40s and 80s—

those perfect stones with their false promise to cut her
　　　pain with their fuzz and blur—the way they do

at her apartment in the projects, a home more makeshift
　　　than her nylon tent with its walls stretched taut,

its strings staked between oak roots. In this quiet,
　　　she sketches her children's faces with charcoal,

applying skills she's learning in community college
　　　art classes. She outlines their curved cheeks,

their almond-shaped eyes, uses long, sweeping strokes
　　　for her daughter's hair, a softer mark for the scar

on her son's chin. Dark comes early beneath the trees.
　　　Without the luxury of electric light, she's learning

how to smudge charcoal, how to block in the mid-tones,
　　　by battery-powered lantern—a small sacrifice

for this shelter of trees when she most misses her kids,
　　　when her brain won't stop buzzing.

Susan Truxell Sauter

These fields

My father's fields
are for sale once again,
available to familial blood.

Crows, cowbirds, and magpies—
marauders all—skim low
over the soybeans
sit in hedges
atop roof ledges
in these fields
where ancestors were conceived
born, killed by chore and toil.

I slow the truck, snap
a drive-by image. With
instinct and against,
I speed on.

Susan Truxell Sauter

Exit sign: Sandusky/Norwalk

Somewhere south of here
answers smolder and dust falls upward.

Somewhere south of here
lie fields of my forefathers.
Hulking metal creatures roll
over soil, gather kernels and cobs
break sift spit out
for the next regeneration;
golden grains emptied
into elevators, memorials
to the gleaning, to the meaning
of any one of our lives.

Bonnie Proudfoot

How Do I Lie Awake
–after Alison Krauss

It is morning in August and it can only be August,
can only be southeastern Ohio where heat
hangs on damp earth, your limbs ache

with the hot weight of sleep, you might as well
be hovering above your tissue paper body,
again, you dream of visiting an old friend,

of the path through woods to her cabin,
how she welcomed you, though she
is no one you have met in this life.

Outside the window, doves coo-oo-oo,
the sun begins to bronze the day, in yards
pink ladies are standing watch on pale stalks,

seeking company but floating alone,
weightless flowers rising like a mirage,
bracing for the sweltering breeze.

Bonnie Proudfoot

Perseids

Tonight the stars keep their distance
We stretch our necks, on our backs
in the bed of the pickup.

We curse the haze, the clouds, the moon
spotlighting the night sky too bright. Out
in the field, horses snort, crickets grind

the minutes away, my son's breath slows
down, he is warm in my arms. At the creek
a bullfrog twangs like a banjo. It starts.

David says whoa, he sees one flash past.
But I was watching a bat shoot out
toward the moon, circle back.

We are surrounded by everything
night, everything softly glowing. A cloud
stipples the moon, dapples into patches.

David sees the next one too. I see
the top of the ridge, medium gray,
the black cutout shapes of trees,

silver mist on the hilltop soft
as smoke. We are low in the bowl
of the sky, slow clouds flow. David sees

the third meteor streaking earthward,
but a whip-poor-will calls and calls.
I have been waiting all my life to rise.

Richard Hague

Goods Not for Sale

It is good to rise in the morning,
in the country, your neighbor's
stove smoke ghosting the shreds of dawn
that silver down through the trees. It is good
to have survived long enough
to know that pain may dwindle in time.
It is good to speak plainly, when life is
sweet water to drink.
It is good to have places like this
to remember when away: old barrels,
tractors rusted a velvet red
in fields of blooming Ironweed,
the glimpse of an Amish girl, her dress like a hanky
waved in the wind, her face full of calm
and light.
                    It is good to wake at midnight
to the song of a mockingbird, or the *harr*
of an owl far over the hill. It is good
to know that thunderstorm can clean the soul.
It is good to have been given
years of homely music: the tinny gripe
of the pump, the snort and gurgle of the sink drain,
the *zee zee zee* pizzicati of katydids
in the cherry tree. It is good
not to owe anything for all of this:
enough to breathe, listen, be.
                    And it is good
not to have lived too long in the country.
One grows old like the trees, and lightning
is waiting. Even the broom sedge, in winter,
cuts at the shins. Frost knocks on the doors
of the knees. The city offers gifts
of crowds and fervor and movement. Stillness can be
fearful. Even the traffic lights' come and go
is an invitation. Shop lights shimmer and bloom,
day winks and goes on.

Even out on the sidewalk, though hustle
hawks its hurry every hour, though
all seems hapless Heraclitean change,
every pigeon, here, now, seems every pigeon ever.

Richard Hague

Chink

Backyard,
this is as small
as the cardinal's *good cheer* gets,
sharp shard of sound
chipped from as-if-frozen air.
Still, if it were to have color
it would be pointed scarlet,
like a splint of fire,
or blue-white
like the flame of acetylene.
If it were music
it would be one high C,
some maestro's hot-headed urge
of his horns.

In the woods,
chink is enough.
Under pine sighs,
near the stony mumble
of the creek,
it speaks everything needed
to cardinal:
Here.
I know you're there.
Listen.

Contributor Statements

Steve Abbott: Columbus sits on U.S. Route 23, immortalized in the phrase I heard from childhood to describe the three R's of the journey of many Appalachian natives: "Readin', Writin' and Route 23." My neighborhood had several Appalachian transplants, and the twang in the voice of my first wife often elicited the question, "What part of the South you from, honey?" To which she always replied, "Southern Ohia." Thirty years of teaching at Columbus State Community College taught me even more about the culture, pride, and struggles of Appalachian students who were the first in their families to attend college.

Heidi Arnold: I am from the eastern region of Ohio in Muskingum County. I was born in Zanesville, a town named after Ebenezer Zane who established a road connecting West Virginia to Ohio and Kentucky. My roots are tied to my father's bicycle shop located near the convergence of the Licking and Muskingum Rivers. My father immersed me in bluegrass music on a hillside of weekend festivals before I learned to write. My grandmother told stories of riding the train to Philippi, West Virginia, to visit her grandparents. And my grandfather took me mushroom hunting in Coshocton County where his family farmed.

Ellen Austin-Li: A northeastern transplant, I've lived in Cincinnati, Ohio, for the past twenty-five years. I have spent years honing my craft in Pauletta Hansel's poetry classes and workshops with Richard Hague and Sherry Cook Stanforth. I have learned much about honoring connection to the land and kin from these writers and the other stellar Ohio Appalachian poets in the many circles where I have been welcomed. I am grateful for the opportunity to raise my voice with the fine poets at whose feet I have learned so much.

Ivars Balkits: I have resided in Appalachian Ohio 26 years, specifically in Athens. I can claim further that I am Appalachian through my birth in Olean, southwestern New York State. In the years I have lived in Athens, I have committed to bettering my community through political activism, sustainable development projects and promotion, and raising awareness about regional history through writing plays and performing monologues about the labor movement here in the 1880s and beyond. I have been involved in the literary and arts scene as well, including co-hosting for 20 years a poetry program on local radio station WOUB AM.

KB Ballentine: I always knew my grandparents were from Ohio, but it wasn't until we took their ashes to Greenlawn Cemetery in Nelsonville that it became apparent how much of my family's history is there. My mother and aunts had to go to the hand-written account to find where my "many-times-great" grandfather, Solomon Smith, purchased plots both there and at Maple Grove in Granville. We placed my grandparents next to Edger Smith (buried 1894). I had considered myself a Florida-child who now lives in and loves the mountains of east Tennessee, but I am excited to discover and explore these Ohio roots.

Tom Barlow: I have lived in Ohio all my life. The family emigrated from Northern England, settling first in Barnesville, Ohio, a Central Appalachian town, where they established a strawberry business. From there, my ancestors worked their way west, first to Quaker City, where Great-great-grandpa Jim was a farrier, then to Cambridge, where great-grandpa Ray mined coal. The family followed the industrial revolution north to Canton but never neglected to put in a large garden and took great pride in being beholden to no one.

Elizabeth Beck: I was born and raised in Youngstown, Ohio. I studied and taught art history and literature in Cincinnati before moving to Lexington, Kentucky, where I have raised my family, taught, written, and made art for the past twenty years, ever interweaving experiences from my Ohio childhood.

Diana Becket: I moved to Ohio in 1989 for work opportunities with my family and raised two children in Cincinnati. I taught composition courses at the University of Cincinnati for twenty-five years and began to write poetry when I retired. I write in a cabin on a creek near Ripley, Ohio. I am a member of a group of writers: Old Washington Wordsmiths. We meet once a month in Washington Hall near Maysville to share poetry and music.

Roy Bentley: Born in Dayton, Ohio, I'm the first generation of my family born out of the eastern Kentucky hills. I guess you could say I "summered" in Kentucky with my grandmother Frances Collier Potter, who educated me in the history and mythology of the Bentleys and Potters, the Bates and Colliers. Both of my parents were born in Neon, Kentucky; Dayton, Ohio, is where they met again and married in 1953. My connection to Appalachia has been deepened and nurtured by my friend Jack Wright who took me back to eastern Kentucky/western Virginia many times through the years.

Ace Boggess: I lived across the river from Ohio for two long stretches of my life. I spent many nights walking beside that river staring out at the far shore. As a young reporter in the 90s, I spent a lot of time in Ohio, covering county fairs, drug busts, and such for *The Herald-Dispatch*, its circulation included in many Ohio counties.

Dianne Borsenik: I'm a first-generation Ohioan, but my Appalachian roots have run deeply through the Dempsey and Keith families in Kanawha County, West Virginia, for generations. In the 1950s, my parents and many of my mother's brothers and sisters moved north to find work in the then-booming Ohio factories. Encouraged by my mother to follow my love of words, I've been reading and writing poetry since I was four years old. My Appalachian roots, which have never been more than four and a half hours' drive away, are forever a part of that which gave birth to "me."

Lee Boyle: I was raised in the small town of East Palestine, Ohio. The Appalachian spirit runs deep within my soul, as I feel a strong connection with the wonderment and beauty which springs from Ohio. I lost my father very young, my little brothers and I being mostly raised by my mother. I have moved back into my childhood home to take care of my mother, a sure recipe for full-circle Ohioan moments. Appalachian life makes me feel at home among kind townsfolk as well as alienated as an artist, a delicious push and pull.

Nancy Susanna Breen: I'd always heard stories about my mother's people in Brown and Clermont Counties, but I was an adult before I realized they gave me Appalachian roots. Living or dead, they always seemed "out there" beyond the city somewhere, not people with a culture of their own. Thanks to Grandma recording herself telling family stories in 1989, the handed-down tales were preserved, at least as she remembered them. Having grown up in Warren County, she thought her Appalachian connection was through her husband's people, but genealogy has shown me she also had roots in Appalachian Ohio.

Kelsey Brown: I grew up in Southern Ohio and spent my college years traveling back and forth from Columbus and Cincinnati along I-71. That highway almost feels as much like home as my current apartment. My father and I spent a lot of time hiking and photographing the more hidden places of Ohio—the caves at Hocking Hills, the seven hills of Cincinnati, and the dog-walking trails all over the state. At one point, I thought I might leave, but I was drawn back by the people more than the scenery, and I still live in Columbus.

Kathleen S. Burgess: The 1900 census identified Grandpa, a seven-year-old orphan in Appalachian Virginia, as a servant. At fourteen he escaped. He walked, working his way across the mountains to Ohio. Grandma, made to leave school early, later married Grandpa at sixteen. They lost their tenant farm in the Depression. Dad, their youngest, injured during WWII, attended college on the GI Bill. This family valued education. My Appalachian husband and I taught public school students—he, history; I, music—in Chillicothe where we've lived three decades.

John Burroughs: I was born on the banks of the Cherry River in Richwood, West Virginia, in 1966. When I was a toddler, Mom and Dad brought me to Ohio where he took a job at the Lorain Ford plant, and I grew up Southern Baptist in Elyria before embarking on my own journeys. But my family visited our hometown several times a year, and much of my heart has remained there.

Joshua Butts: My hometown is Jackson, Ohio, a small town in the Appalachian foothills. Though I grew up doing traditional rural activities, like hunting and fishing, I also played in punk bands and was a skateboarder. I would spend time playing in Horse Creek with cousins, but with those same kids would walk to see the new bypass being built, the bypass a metaphor for something that is here that can also take one away. I am proud of my complex Appalachian roots that delight in storytelling and strangeness found at the permeable border of ruralness and the wider world.

Shuly Xóchitl Cawood: I grew up in the village of Yellow Springs, Ohio, a town surrounded by soybean and corn fields. My father hails from Harlan, Kentucky, and my mother is from Aguascalientes, Mexico, so my youth was a delightful mix. I live in Johnson City, Tennessee, now, but I'm still a small-town Ohio girl, happy I was raised in a town where it was normal to hear people ring cowbells at football games. My heart will always be in Ohio.

Leslie Clark: My mother and I moved to Cincinnati, Ohio, in 1958, but I was born in Fairmont, West Virginia. My father and his parents were born there. I lived with my mother and my maternal grandparents for five years in Fairmont. I received unconditional love, was cherished, and learned how to become a strong, independent woman. I recall standing by a window with my mom, watching a storm, and hearing her whisper, "Can you smell the rain?" I will always be tethered to those mountains, trees, and the smell of rain. I go back to visit West Virginia whenever I can.

Hattie Sells Clarke: I was born and lived most of my early life in the flat, flat center of the state of Ohio, surrounded by corn fields, raspberry gardens, and gravel side roads. I went to college in the northern part of the state. There were impressive snowfalls and maple festivals. When my children were small, we moved to the southeastern part of Ohio, where there are low hills and two rivers knotted together. My grown children have left home, of course, and have traveled, but they always come back to southeastern Ohio.

James Cochran: I was born on a farm in the rolling green foothills of Appalachian Ohio. The farm has been in my family since the late 1800s, long enough to put down roots that have sustained and nourished six generations of us. I have often felt conflicted or reluctant to claim myself as Appalachian, or felt I never completely fit in. Through writing, I feel the deep power in embracing and exploring my origins, especially in these times when our national character feels increasingly uprooted and transitory. I feel a deep gratitude to my parents for keeping our family in these sheltering hills, even when times were not easy.

Alan Cohen: I grew up in a suburb of St. Louis and after college taught in the inner city of Chicago. After a move to the spectacular Hocking Hills in 1972, I bought a home. Settling on an old abused hill farm, I rolled up miles of barbed wire, built a house, planted thousands of trees, created many gardens, and learned my greatest lessons from the land itself.

Rita Coleman: My parents and older brother were born in Monroe County, Tennessee, and came North after World War II for a better life. I am first-born Ohioan. Our yearly family vacations took us South every August to visit aunts, uncles, and cousins, most of them sharecroppers in watermelon and tobacco. I grew up on green beans and cornbread, and weekend breakfasts always included biscuits and gravy. Ten years ago, I discovered I was not unique and found others just as proud of their heritage as I am of mine.

Jessica Cory: On my father's side, I am a seventh-generation Appalachian Ohioan with most of my family living in Frankfort, Ohio, over the years. The Corys were (and some still are) primarily farmers in the region. My dad's cousin Joe and his wife Terri run the oldest working farm in Ross County, Ohio, which was started by Nathan Cory in 1798, and my grandfather Robert Cory, who got his start growing produce and running fruit stands, still operates Cory's Wildflower Gardens despite being in his mid-90s. I lived in Ross County until 2010, when I moved to North Carolina, where I live today, growing tomatoes, green beans, and corn to honor my relatives.

Elaine Costanzo: Born in Ohio, I grew up in Northern Virginia. My sister and I spent a month each summer on our grandparents' Appalachian retirement farm. We roamed the hills, rode ponies, and swam in the Wakatomika Creek. The sounds of bleating sheep and pumping oil wells and the smells of apple orchard, barn, and haymow formed our backdrop, seeped into our beings. Marriage and a job for my New Jersey husband brought me back to this very same county in Ohio. I had returned to the hills of my childhood. I've lived here for over forty years. Serendipity made me an Appalachian.

Ed Davis: A West Virginia native, I was pleased to find "another Appalachia" when I transplanted to Ohio in 1976, to teach at, first, Wright State University, then Sinclair

Community College in Dayton. I developed and taught Appalachian Folkways at Sinclair, helping students connect with their roots. Also, my connection to the Arc of Appalachia land preservation organization deepened my understanding and appreciation for Central Appalachia.

Mary Lucille DeBerry: During my childhood, I spent most summers in Cincinnati, where through most of WWII my uncle was in the U.S. Corps of Engineers— followed by employment with steel companies. In the 1950s he transferred to ORMET where, on a farm near Woodsfield, I observed a very different lifestyle in a hardscrabble rural area. In the mid-1960s, I worked for two years at WSTV-TV (Now WTOV-TV) in Steubenville. These three immersive views of Ohio— a big city with many Appalachian immigrants; a rural area with a small county seat; and a medium size town—each provided me with treasured memories.

Robert DeMott: Though I was born in Connecticut and raised there, I have lived in southeastern Ohio since 1969, when I accepted a teaching position in the English Department of Ohio University, where I taught for 44 years. I consider this part of Ohio to be home for myself and my family. The geography, the culture, the environment, the values, and the people, have entered much of my work in poetry and prose.

Cindy Dubielak: I moved to southeastern Ohio from northwestern Ohio in 1983 to attend Ohio University in the Creative Writing Program. I've lived here ever since. I have worked in the local food co-op, been active in local arts organizations, got married, raised two sons and a step-daughter, and ended a marriage after addiction and mental illness took it over. I taught older than average students at a local college for 25 years and learned a lot about grit. I'm proud to have survived and attribute my survival to the close knit friendships and must-do reality of Appalachian Ohio and its people, of which I consider myself one.

Cathryn Essinger: I live in Southwest Ohio, in the Ohio River Valley, along the edge of Appalachia. I am surrounded by Appalachian voices, from my favorite grocery store clerk who tells me about medicinal uses for herbs, to my friend Vivian, who left Kentucky as a child. She became a well known academic voice throughout the US, but today she still writes weekly newspaper columns about growing up in Appalachia. I live in Troy, Ohio where I write about conservation, raise Monarch butterflies, and try to live up to my dog's expectations.

Terry Focht: I was born in Dayton, Ohio, but spent many summers with my uncle in the mountains of Eastern Kentucky and also the Ohio River Valley. Many of my best memories came from those summers exploring nature and listening to the stories of my extended family and discovering my grandmas' Appalachian roots. As a young boy I was always looking to explore paths where Daniel Boone might have traveled. I lived in Kentucky, with my wife, Jan, twenty more years and five years near the Great Smokey Mountains in Tennessee before retiring and returning to Ohio.

Lynette Ford: Born in Mercer County in Appalachian Pennsylvania at the border of Ohio, I was raised in the smoke of train engines, coal furnaces and steel mills. I spent summers with my great-grandparents in East Liverpool, Ohio. Once a place of busy pottery plants, industrial transport via rail and on the Ohio River, it is now a city struggling to survive. The old neighborhoods no longer exist, but their memories, and the wooded hills and river valleys that also defined them, remain touchpoints in my life and work as a fourth-generation, Affrilachian storyteller and writer.

Sylvia Freeman: I live in North Carolina. My sister attended the Cincinnati Conservatory of Music and I visited her frequently while she was a student. I went to my first opera at the zoo, met lots of her friends and my future brother-in-law and his family there. My niece still lives there. I have so many fond memories of Ohio.

Jane Ann Fuller: I was born and raised in Logan, Ohio, county seat of Hocking County, population around 7,000. I raised my kids and worked here my entire adult life. I am the descendent of river boat gamblers, horse thieves, hog farmers, and coal miners. My ancestors founded Marietta, and my parents took us kids to Campus Martius to show us the Devol's in the museum. That was quite the thrill as a child. Not long ago I started lessons on fiddle with the famous Liz Shaw. I chose fiddle because of dad's life-long love of Old Time and Blue Grass music.

David Garrison: While I was born in Bremerton, Washington, I have lived in Dayton, Ohio, since 1979, and my grandparents were from Ohio and Kentucky. My paternal grandfather and grandmother were from Mansfield, Ohio, and my maternal grandmother was from Franklin, Kentucky. They would say things like, "I was just fixin' to do that," and I have absorbed many such speech patterns and ways of looking at the world from them. My Kentucky grandmother made the best fried chicken I have ever tasted.

Matthew Gilbert: I am a Tennessee Appalachian poet whose best friend lives in Ohio. I am intrigued by how alike, yet distinguishable Ohio Appalachia is to my own lived experience. I have lived in several Appalachian states, and I love how nature, location, and culture are connected. There is deep reliance on landscape to maintain historical connections to the past, especially in the eastern coast of Ohio, where people continue to carry on traditional events, memories, and celebrations. As a Tennessean, this is an experience that makes me feel at home yet welcomes me to open up and see the world through a new lens.

Susan F. Glassmeyer: My mother's side of the family journeyed across the Ohio River from Kentucky and made their lives here in Ohio. I come from bricklayers, railroad folks, heavy smokers, drinkers, gamblers, rabble-rousers, names like Hank and Irma. From do as you're told, beat the rug, hold your tongue, and over my dead body. My work is also informed by the rich narratives told to me by clients of Ohio Appalachian origin in my somatic practice at the Holistic Health Center of Cincinnati.

Jonathan Graham: Born an Ohioan along the river in Martins Ferry, I breathed air that chugged from smokestacks at Wheeling Steel and grew up not far from there in a small enclave of immigrant Slovak coal miners in the foothills of the Appalachian Mountains. Except for being drafted into the military during the Vietnam War and receiving formal education in South Carolina, I have lived in Ohio's Appalachian region my entire life, residing for the past 35 years on a farm near the village of Zoar in rural Tuscarawas County. I know about pawpaw fruit, the fiddle and the scythe.

Connie Green: I am an Appalachian native (born in Grant Town, West Virginia) and have lived in the Appalachian region all my life. I attended Denison University (Granville, Ohio) and maintain contact with the university through annual contributions and through Ohio friends from college. Having spent my young years in the coal mining area of southeastern Kentucky, I had aunts and uncles who migrated to Ohio during World War II in search of work. My father, who was working as a coal miner, moved the family to Oak Ridge, Tennessee, during the war, an area where I still live.

Susan Grimm: I have lived in Ohio all of my life. My connection to Appalachia is much more tentative although my father's family did come from West Virginia. The landscape/ neighborhoods of Cleveland (mostly) wallpaper my poems although pride of place is usually given over to Lake Erie which delights me with its sparkle and slaps me with its waves.

Jeff Gundy: For more than half my life, I've lived in the flatlands of northwest Ohio, but made frequent forays into the hills and valleys to the east and south—the Cuyahoga Valley, the Clifton Gorge, the river town of Martins Ferry, the rolling farmlands and gritty cities east of Mansfield where my son and his family have put down roots. Those places and their people have worked their way into my poems, sometimes openly, sometimes covertly, as the world works itself into us, whether we notice or not.

Kari Gunter-Seymour: I am a ninth generation Appalachian. My people, Welsh, Irish, Dutch, have lived, worked, prayed and died within Appalachia's borders. I am so grateful to my ancestors, all those generations, who worked the land, the mines, served their country, a few going off to the factories, never giving up—from Virginia to North Carolina, down into South Carolina, up and across to Tennessee and finally southeastern Ohio. Needless to say, I come from feisty stock. It's their voices I hear as I write and, more often than not, their stories I tell.

Richard Hague: I am a fifth-generation Northern Appalachian from Steubenville, Ohio. My great-great grandfather, Theodore Butler, worked as a riverman on the Ohio as early as 1840, making many trips from Pittsburgh to New Orleans. My maternal great-grandmother Cora Woods Davis was born, according to family lore, "somewhere in West Virginia." Her daughter, Maude Mae Davis Heights, helped establish one of the first day-care centers for working women in the country in downtown Steubenville. I have spent many of my adult summers rusticating and running the ridges from a camp in Monroe County, Ohio, a few miles west of the Ohio River.

Jennifer Hambrick: I am an Ohio native and longtime resident with deep ties to Appalachia on both sides of my family. My mother's father and paternal grandparents (and multi-great-grandparents) lived in Berea, Kentucky (Madison County) for generations. One of my great-grandfathers helped found Berea College. My great-grandmother was the subject of the photograph by noted photographer Doris Ulmann that inspired my poem "Hands." My mother's mother and maternal great-grandparents lived in Laurel County, Kentucky, on the farm that inspired my attached poem "Roots." My mother, herself an Appalachian poet, was born and raised in Winchester, Kentucky (Clark County).

William Scott Hanna: My maternal-side roots stretch far back into Ohio to the early

1800's when the Robeson family came from Cumberland, Maryland and settled in Knox County, and then later moved to establish a family farm in Coshocton County sometime in the 1890's. One of fourteen children, my grandfather moved his family from Coshocton to Canton, Ohio where much of the family still resides. I have lived my whole life in the Upper Ohio Valley and currently reside in St. Clairsville, Ohio in Belmont County.

Pauletta Hansel: I migrated to Cincinnati from southeastern Kentucky in 1979, riding the tail of the great migration from the coal fields to the city. I came for school, and stayed for work. My mother's relatives still live near the Revolutionary War land grant which brought them to Kentucky, though it was sold to the coal company for a half-dollar an acre several generations ago. My father's family were more recent immigrants, not arriving in Appalachia until after 1800. My writing and I claim dual citizenship in the large urban Appalachian community and in the Appalachian literary community which spans the region.

Hayley Mitchell Haugen: When I moved from Los Angeles, California, to Athens, Ohio, in 2001 to pursue my Ph.D. in American Literature, I had no inkling of the outstanding Appalachian poets who were to become my mentors, colleagues, and closest friends. But we poets, we find our tribes quite naturally, and my own tribe's circle widened exponentially when I founded *Sheila-Na-Gig online* and Sheila-Na-Gig Editions. Through my efforts as an editor and publisher it's been a joy to support the work of some of Appalachia's finest poets.

Melissa Helton: I was born and raised in Toledo, Ohio, to an American and an immigrant. I spent my summers in southern Ohio through childhood. Once I had a family of my own, I moved to my husband's Appalachian Kentucky to raise those kids in the mountains. The family splits their time between Kentucky and Ohio. I have driven up and down I-75 more times than could possibly be counted. Since the cardinal is the state bird for both homes, it is one of my favorite birds.

Michael Henson: Back when Blue Creek, a little crossroads town in Adams County, still had a school, I came there, fresh out of college, to teach. My teaching didn't last long, but my ties to Adams County and its people did. There I met some of the best storytellers, and best truth-tellers I have known. I never got to live there again, but still visit as often as I can. The stories have often been sad and the truths hard but necessary.

Donna Hilbert: I was born in Grandfield, Oklahoma, a red dirt, almost-town near the Texas border, but my grandmother, Virginia May Burke Zumwalt was born and raised in Virginia. I have a dear friend who is a third-generation Ohio Appalachian, and this poem makes me think of her. I think that might be why we became friends, that first-memory language forged in Appalachia. Scotch-Irish, Methodist, Democrat, Appalachian—born that way, die that way, my grandmother always said.

Kevin Hoskinson: I am the son of Harry and Doris (Howell) Hoskinson, who spent their early lives in rural Woodsfield, Ohio. They married in later years after World War II. Both were from poor farming families whose lives were shaped by the Great Depression. From Woodsfield, they relocated to the Lorain, Ohio, area where Harry found work in the steel mill. I teach at Lorain County Community College in Elyria, Ohio, and live in Berea, Ohio, with my wife, Alicia.

Teagan Hughes: Being from Appalachian Ohio has always been a fact of life for me; I didn't think about it much growing up. I grew up in Athens, Ohio, and I have family from Portsmouth and Manchester. Moving away for college changed my perspective. Suddenly, I was surrounded by peers who seemed to forget that I could exist among them, with some being openly condescending towards Appalachia and Ohio both. Being in this new environment caused me to form a deeper connection with Appalachian Ohio, as I learned to take it with me wherever I go.

Clarissa Jakobsons: Weekends, poets gathered yearly at Mark Jordan's Malabar Hostel in the Appalachian Plateau foothills of Lucas, Ohio to celebrate the landscape. Louis Bromfield's home was nearby. Unfortunately, the park closed these doors. Today, I share poems formed from wonderful memories.

Mitchell James: After living the first twenty-five years of my life in rural locations in Illinois, Arkansas, and South Dakota, I lived nearly a decade in rural Appalachia and have for the past six years lived in Northeast Ohio. It's a bit different up here. I miss the country and mountains, but the Great Lakes region has its own beauty and draw.

Keri Johnson: To say that I am from Appalachia is an understatement; I am of it. Both sides of my family have lived in Appalachia before it was named; my mother's side were settlers of Gallia and Lawrence counties; my dad's side, pre-North Carolinians turned Kentuckians turned Southeast Ohioans. My relationship with Appalachia is a relationship I have with myself; ever-changing, ever-blossoming, ever-present. I didn't realize this until I met people who weren't like me. None of this is to say the hills are mine, but they are me. Within them will always rest my people, our stories, and myself.

William Jolliff: My family settled in Ohio early in the nineteenth century. I was born in Delaware County and reared there on our family farm. After leaving at 18, I lived in Athens County, Sandusky County, Erie County, Ashland County, and Franklin County (where I did graduate work at Ohio State). Though I moved to Oregon for work thirty years ago, much of my poetry is still set in Ohio and on that farm.

Mark Jordan: I am the son of parents who came north to Ohio from the hills of eastern Kentucky looking for work. Descendants of generations of Appalachian farmers, they wanted something different and joined the exodus to the industrial cities of the Midwest. Today their son is a historian, poet, music critic, and playwright. I have learned to treasure my heritage. I left the city and moved into Appalachian Ohio because no matter how grand my adventures get, I still only feel at home among the hills.

Jeremy Jusek: I was born in Ohio and lived here my entire life. I have close and distant relatives in West Virginia, Virginia, and North Carolina. Any vacations we took growing up were with family or in cabins throughout the rural East Coast, and much of my love of Nature was formed while hiking through the Smoky Mountains, the Metroparks, Wayne National Forest, and Hocking Hills. My preference for America's wild, and the people who live there, are a permanent part of my identity—despite having spent the last decade in the suburbs.

Jackie Kalbli: I am a second-generation Appalachian migrant. My parents came to Southwest Ohio from Elliott County, Kentucky, in 1951, the year I was born. They came because there was no work in the hollers, but they brought the hollers with them in sounds and words. As a young child, I spoke the language of the mountains. Then in school, I learned it was the language of hillbillies and briar-hoppers. That meant ignorant. I learned to roll my words out flat and speak properly. I had lost my heritage. I want my voice back!

Jennifer Schomburg Kanke: My parents were originally from Scioto County, so although I grew up in Columbus, I spent most summers and holidays in New Boston and Minford. From the ages of 15-25, I played washtub bass and pennywhistle in an old-time string band with my parents. I lived in Athens for six years while attending Ohio University and then moved back the next year. I then lived for two years in Athens before moving to Lottridge, which is halfway between Guysville and Coolville, which are halfway between Athens and Parkersburg. I lived there for seven years before moving to Florida in 2010.

Kenneth Armitage Kawaji: My father's family is from the Menifee and Clark county area of eastern Kentucky. Relatives range from Mt. Sterling, Winchester, Grant's Lick, Owensboro in Western Kentucky. My grandfather followed the work from the coal mines north to the steel mills in Middleton, Ohio. I crewed on the Delta Queen when it was home ported out of Cincinnati.

Sean Kelbley: Born in Nelsonville, I've lived in southeastern Ohio almost all my life. Appalachia is sometimes portrayed as a place to escape from, and as a younger person, that was my plan. But four years in the flatlands of metropolitan Columbus taught me that I'm just no good without hills. Today I live with my husband in a house we built on his family's Meigs County farm, work as a primary school counselor, and write when I can. Perhaps because it's been a process for me to recognize and fully appreciate home, the concept often pops up in my poems.

Diane Kendig: I was born and raised in Canton, Ohio, and only recently realized that both sides of my family originally "settled" in Appalachian counties, though they were pretty unsettled. My paternal Pennsylvania Dutch grandparents left Lancaster, Pennsylvania, for East Rochester to farm with their 13 children, but like many Depression era farmers, lost the farm and moved, living pillar to post in Canton and Massillon. My maternal grandparents, Scottish and Welsh miners, came in the early 1900s to mine here in Ohio, and all their children, including the grandfather of this poem, moved to the city and eventually found other work.

Stephanie Kendrick: I have always lived in Appalachian Ohio, and because of this, have always felt the tension of identity within our region. Too north to be Southern, too midwest to be Northern, too south to be Midwestern. In more ways than one I have had to elbow my way into a room, or into a seat at a table because of where I am from. So I write about place; the beauty of our region is sacred and the complexities of our people is just the same. I always hope to honor both as honestly as I can.

C.F. Kinney: I have lived in Appalachian Ohio on and off since I was a toddler. I feel a deep connection to the land and local nature. Much of my childhood was spent outdoors in the woods. Some of my best memories involve searching for trilliums and Dutchman's breeches in spring; trading calls with friendly cardinals; and, in winter, watching the UPS driver put chains on his tires before braving icy local hills.

Ben Kline: A crick rat from the floodplain cornfields of Lawrence County's west side, where the Ohio runs north, I grew up on my family's hay fields, building fence through summer, working the sawmill in winter. Currently in Cincinnati, I often write poems and fictions about the tall tales and intrigue of my Appalachian upbringing.

Kip Knott: All throughout my childhood and adolescence, I spent whole summers living with my grandparents in the coal mining ghost town of Hemlock, Ohio, located in the foothills of Northern Appalachia. My grandfather had worked the mines for 13 years until an explosion seriously injured him and forced him and my grandmother to relocate to Columbus to find work. After 25 years, they retired and moved back to Hemlock and the house they had built on weekends. The time I spent living with them was the best education I ever received. Every night at the dinner table was a lesson in storytelling, and I would absorb every word about working the mines, about farming, about life in the factory, and about surviving no matter what life throws at you.

Sandra Kolankiewicz: I have lived in southeastern Ohio for almost fifty years with a few international forays. Wherever I went, the hills called to me and brought me back.

Mark Kuhar: In 1936, my uncle, George Kuhar, graduated from Ohio University. In 1950, my father graduated from Ohio University. I got my first taste of Athens in 1972 when I attended an athletic camp on campus. I subsequently attended and graduated in 1980. All three of my kids also found their way to Athens (two graduates and one still on campus.) Athens, and the surrounding area, are like a second home to us. Over the years, the people, the places, the areas surrounding Athens, the smells and sounds, history and geography, all have a magical appeal to me.

Becca J.R. Lachman: Living in Athens County, Ohio for the past 16 years has changed the way I see others, my body, and the land around me—now I want to marvel in and protect all three, though I (mostly) accept that I can't control them. It's here I've claimed names with both hands: "student," "poet," "endo warrior," "foster mom." I mourn the years when our pawpaw grove bears no fruit, and my house is filled with vases, recipes, and books gifted by local mentors, gone for years now. I write and sing and mother and fight on, in good part, because of them.

Kevin LeMaster: I have lived in northeastern Kentucky most of my life, with a fifteen year stint in a town called Beaver in what is still considered Southern Ohio. Not only was I born in Ohio, but I have worked mainly in Ohio throughout my entire professional/not professional career. The Appalachian area means a lot to me, and I am proud to be part of its heritage.

Brooklyn Lengyel: People have always had trouble pronouncing my last name. Any time I have to say it aloud to someone so they can write it down, I always spell it before they get a chance to ask. Lengyel is a Hungarian word meaning Polish, which wraps together nicely in one word the complicated history of my family. My great-great grandfather left Hungary in the 1940s, a wise decision considering our Jewish ancestry. Because of him, I have always lived in Appalachia. I've always lived in these mountains, and without them and my grandfather's decision, I may not even be here today.

Cathy Cultice Lentes: I am a Buckeye native who has lived in the hills of Appalachia for over 30 years on an old wooded farm with creeks running full of tales and poetry. When not writing, reading, or taking photographs along the winding Ohio River, I work in the Meigs Local School District, supporting students with special needs and spreading the joy of literature to whomever will listen.

Denton Loving: My family is from both the northern and southern areas of Appalachia. This is uncomfortable for some people who want to define Appalachia in very narrow terms, usually in ways that only fit their own backgrounds. There are many in Ohio's Appalachian region who can relate to this conundrum of being told they can't be one if they're the other. As a writer and editor, I've worked with many artists who clearly know it's possible to be both Ohioan and Appalachian. As a publisher, it's been my distinct pleasure to provide spaces for the work of writers from this often-overlooked region.

Marjorie Maddox: The roots of place grow deep. Although I was born and raised in Columbus, my parents' familial connections led to windy excursions into Appalachian Ohio. My father, who grew up in Chillicothe and Portsmouth and earned Eagle Scout at a young age, instigated adventure after adventure. My maternal aunt packed us up in her VW Camper and off we went to the hills. My great-grand uncle, baseball legend Branch Rickey, grew up in Duck Run and, at 17, taught at a one-room schoolhouse in Turkey Creek.

John C. Mannone: I lived in Ohio for several years when I worked as a consulting nuclear engineer, but my permanent residence is in East Tennessee.

Preston Martin: My parents were born in Winchester, Adams Country, Ohio, in the summer of 1916. The farm where my mother grew up was in the family until just five years ago; for almost 70 years I returned to that little town and 33 acre farm. Though I never lived there, it was forever home. I grew up outside the northern Appalachia steel towns of Youngstown and Steubenville. There we snuck into strip mines to drive cars and drink beer. I received an undergraduate degree in Athens. Many of my poems are centered on the farm, twenty miles up from the river.

Barbara McCullough: After 38 years in West Virginia, I moved to settle in Marietta along the Ohio River. Between the two states, I've discovered what Appalachia is and is not, what Appalachia may or may not become. Yet, this rich river town life assures that Appalachia lets me keep moving: college greens, Great Lakes, wind and solar power farms to the north, rolling corn fields shoulder to shoulder with coal and fracture sites to the east, southern roads through scenic national parks and forests rich with hunting and fishing, and urban interstate highways to both escape and return home to the west.

Jonie McIntire: In high school, I applied to three colleges: one in Ithaca, one in Yellow Springs, and Ohio University in Athens. In the last couple of years, I have had the incredible fortune to stumble onto a group of poets based in Athens, Ohio who feel just like family to me. And it makes me wonder what could have been.

R McNiece: Down yonder near Barlow, Ohio, I heard my calling at ten years old during vacation Bible Camp at Grandma Zelma's church. The white clapboard Layman Methodist rose from a ridge on Route 550 between Marietta and Athens, foundation stone carved and set in 1901. Creek music trickled a holler nearby. I walked the dirt road from Grandma's corn farm every summer morning to fetch well water, just as my old man had done, pumping heavy cast-iron arm, water gushing cold on teeth.

Wendy McVicker: I have been living in southeastern Ohio for more than half my life. The wooded green hills, rivers, and streams have become my home, and the deep-rooted people who live here have nourished my heart. I don't know what kind of poetry I would be writing if I were in a northern city, like the one where I was born, but the cadences, the language, the concerns would undoubtedly lead me to sing in another key. I am grateful that chance brought me here as a "trailing spouse," and that this place took me in. My roots take hold.

Jean Mikhail: I was a college student at Ohio University, when lo and behold, I found Appalachia on a backroad. Riding these foothills on a bicycle, I stopped and looked deeply. I joined an Old Time Fiddle Band and bought a farmhouse where the barn was about 1000 times bigger than the house. I sold it to move closer to town, but I still look out those windows when I write. I have the unique perspective of raising two Guatemalan-born kids here and a biological child. Their experiences are part of my unique perspective of what it means to be from Appalachia.

Barbara Marie Minney: My father spent his whole life trying to escape his Appalachian roots. I did the same until I met Kari Gunter-Seymour who taught me that my Appalachian roots are something to be celebrated. I was born in West Virginia, but at the age of fifteen my family moved to Cadiz, Ohio. Cadiz is the birthplace of Clark Gable, and coal was king. My brother and I roamed the reclaimed coal fields and fished in the strip ponds, and I graduated from Cadiz High School in 1971. My parents spent the rest of their lives in Eastern Ohio.

Penelope Moffet: I was born in Lorain, Ohio. Subsequently, my family moved to California, then Nigeria, before moving to Athens, Ohio. Although we later returned to California and stayed there, I have such vivid memories of those years in Athens. Images from that area rise persistently in my poems. My parents were both also born in Ohio. The family connections to the Buckeye state are strong.

Daniel Edward Moore: I spent my childhood summers in Slocum Station and Minford, Ohio at my grandparents homes. It was the most beautiful, liberating and imaginative time for a young boy from Florida to be able to run the hills, make forts, and just be so radically alive in nature and have it emotionally matched by the incredible love of my family. It will forever shape who I am.

Julie L. Moore: Although I grew up in south Jersey, where every town is basically a suburb of Philly and the Appalachian Trail is a popular destination, I have spent the majority of my adulthood in Ohio on the cusp of Appalachia's other side. I've often hiked in places such as Peebles, Hillsboro, Hocking Hills, and Gallipolis, where my parents later lived for twenty years. I even ziplined in Hocking Hills after I turned 50 to prove to myself I still had it in me to tackle a brand new adventure. Though I now live in Indiana, I love Ohio's Appalachian area.

Robin Mullet: I came to the edge of Appalachia here in Coshocton County 20 years ago. My husband was raised in this county and we returned in our retirement. People here both amaze me—the deep family ties, resiliency through hard times, willingness to pitch in and help—and frustrate me—the ties to extractive industries, the distrust of all things government, resistance to change. But the one constant is the lush hillsides, the fog in the valley, the critters, the beauty that is Appalachia. I am home.

Deni Naffziger: I was raised in Ohio's Appalachian Steel Valley, just outside of Youngstown, Ohio. I earned a BFA in Creative Writing from Bowling Green State University and an MA in Literature with an emphasis in Creative Writing from Ohio University. I have lived in Athens County, Ohio, for over 30 years. My work has been directly influenced by the geography of this place and by early mentors including the poet, Hollis Summers. Athens County is home to a very diverse collection of artists, writers, and musicians, and I have enjoyed a lot of opportunities to collaborate with many of them.

Karen Whittington Nelson: I am from Southeastern Ohio, the first spoiled grandchild of my dad's large family. My relatives covered the shifts at the factories and mills around the Y City, and our lives revolved around Payday. I grew up happy in a little blue-collar community that would never have been mistaken for a suburb, although we lived beyond town and just shy of the fields. My somewhere-in-between-point-of-view grants me the pleasure to choose to top off my truth with a hard point or to erase and edit it into what may have been, had every day been a payday.

Elaine Fowler Palencia: My paternal grandparents, William Clarence Fowler and Lillie Faye Friel, were born in Lawrence County. Both taught in one-room schools before they eloped to Catlettsburg, Kentucky, in 1912 and settled across the river in West Virginia. Many of our people are in Good Hope Cemetery in Gallia County, Ohio, including my Uncle Daryl. I attended Fowler reunions near Gallipolis on the farm of my great-aunt and great-uncle, Mary Frances Fowler Rose and Smelzer Rose. I often use stories about the Ohio Fowlers, Friels, Moores, and Kearnses in my writing. From eastern Kentucky, I've worked in Middletown, an out-migration destination city.

Jacob Phillis: My great-great-grandfather, William Morgan Mathews, was born in 1862, somewhere in southeastern Ohio. William was a schoolteacher who taught at a school in Salt Run. Being poor, like many, William was also in the moonshine business. However, William would get lead poisoning from a bad batch of moonshine and have to be buried at our family cemetery. I was born in 2003 and currently live on Buckingham Ridge (a road located outside of New Alexandria, Ohio), and I continue to overlook the town of Brilliant, Ohio. I have lived in the area for seventeen, going on eighteen years.

David B. Prather: I've spent my entire life as a child of two states: West Virginia and Ohio. Who I am today was built by Appalachia—running the hills of both states as a young man, teaching English and Literature and Writing on both sides of the Ohio River, watching rainstorms drift along the Ohio to stitch together the fabric of my existence. I've had the honor of being an editor for publications in both Ohio and West Virginia as well. The river flows right down the middle of my heart.

Dale Marie Prenatt: I live on top of a mountain in Cincinnati. Where I'm from is Buffalo Creek, West Virginia by way of east Kentucky. As a girl I spent summers with my cousins in western Pennsylvania. My early life was colored by the activities of the

Appalachian literary movement. At Morehead State, I studied poetry and earned a BA in Theatre. A member of the Southern Appalachian Writers Cooperative, I also support Cincinnati's Urban Appalachian Community Coalition. I am a student of our region's stories and ongoing struggle for environmental and social justice.

Bonnie Proudfoot: I crossed the Ohio River in 1996 to attend Ohio University for a PhD in Creative Writing. I was drawn to Athens by the beautiful countryside, and by OU's Lit Fest as well as the *Ohio Review*. Before completing my degree, I began teaching at Hocking College in Nelsonville. I came to recognize that students gave me as much, if not more, than I could give them. Though I no longer teach, I still reside outside Athens, Ohio, with my songwriter husband Dan.

Holli Rainwater: My husband and I moved to Coshocton County in 1994. We both have deep Appalachian roots but spent our growing up years in the suburbs. We wanted our sons to grow up in a place where they could roam in the woods, play in the creek, and eat apples right off the tree. And now our granddaughters get to follow this same path. It's been my great pleasure to spend my career exploring the human story and providing lifelong learning experiences for the Coshocton community.

Michael Rainwater: I was born in White Eyes Township, in Coshocton County, Ohio, the indigenous land of the Lenape people, close to the heart of what we now call the Allegheny Plateau. I grew up roaming the creeks and strip mines of my backyard, and through my mother and grandmother, fell in love with the folklore and music of this region I call home. A carpenter and apple farmer by trade, and descended from a long line of tobacco farmers, mill hands, and mountaineers, I'm happy to work, walk, and write this land, and plan to do so for a long time.

Phoebe Reeves: I grew up in the foothills of the Adirondacks, upstate New York, but transplanted myself to southern Ohio in 2006, to teach at the University of Cincinnati's Clermont College. I teach writing and literature to first-generation college students, run a poetry reading series, and write a lot about my garden. Although I am not native to the Appalachian region, my time here has built a deep connection between my art, my daily living, and the geography of this place. The rural roots I've grown here connect back to the experiences of my childhood, and the snowier mountains of the north.

Erica Reid: I was born and raised in suburbs around Cincinnati, Ohio, but grew up hearing stories about my grandfather's Appalachian childhood in Harlan, Kentucky, where wild turkeys would chase him along his walk home from school. I currently live in Colorado, but my heart, and much of my writing, remains in Ohio and Kentucky.

L. Renée: Mountains, plants, and dirt made me possible. I was born and raised in Columbus, Ohio, the daughter of a West Virginian-born mother whose family migrated to Ohio when she was in middle school after coal money dried up; the granddaughter of a miner who worked 43 years in coal camps across McDowell County, West Virginia, and ultimately died of Black Lung; and the great-granddaughter of a Southwest Virginia tobacco farmer who traded one kind of dirt for another in the mines. I come from proud, Black Appalachians, with a deep abiding love for faith, fried anything, and family.

Louise Robertson: I grew up on the east side of Appalachia but have spent the time since then seeing life from the west side of the mountains. I try to serve my community by making sure there is a stage for the many poetic voices found in Central Ohio as well as working on contributing my own voice to that chorus. A resident of Ohio for over 25 years, I live with my family and two more cats than I ever thought I would have.

Sarah Robinson: My upbringing included growing up on the Ohio River, when my family moved from The Virginia Highlands to the northern panhandle of West Virginia in the mid-sixties. My father worked as a maintenance supervisor at the Cardinal Plant in Brilliant, Ohio, and was locked inside the plant during a contentious strike by the union workers. I am a graduate of Caron Foundations' recovery program. My work reflects my new life.

Barbara Lyghtel Rohrer: For eight years, I was wife to a man in Highland County, a spit away from Serpent Mound. We lived in an old white farmhouse. All that remains of that time, like the daffodils that still bloom in front of the empty log cabin across the field, are memories: hatching baby chicks, planting squash and beans, canning tomatoes, putting up dill pickles, selling honey from our hives, driving country roads in the old black truck, feeding wood burning stoves, baking apple pies, singing to his dulcimer playing, reading Foxfire books, watching the moon rise above the wooded hills.

Peggy Rowan: My mother was raised in a holler in Carter County, Kentucky. My father was from Paintsville, Kentucky. He worked a coal mine until he married my mother and they moved us to Columbus, Ohio, to escape the poverty they grew up in. Growing up we spent a lot of time with my grandparents in the holler until my grandmother passed when I was in high school. I was ashamed of my roots, but now I am proud to be a daughter of Appalachia.

Barbara Sabol: My roots are lodged deep in the rough landscape of southwestern Pennsylvania—Allegheny Mountain steel and coal country. I came to appreciate the culture and values of my blue-collar life only years after a one-way bus ticket carried me far from my home town: Washington, Boston, North Carolina, and finally to northeastern Ohio, a sister rust-belt region. I now call both the rolling hills of Ohio and the Allegheny's hogback ridges home.

Charles Salmons: I am a native of south Columbus, Ohio, an area of the city populated predominantly by Appalachians and their descendants. My grandparents hailed from southeastern Ohio, West Virginia, and Kentucky, and both of my parents were born and spent part of their childhoods in West Virginia. I experienced much of my childhood roaming the hills of Hamlin, West Virginia—also the home of Chuck Yeager, my boyhood hero—and especially my uncle's small farm in Vinton County, Ohio, where our family reunions were held for many years. These places fostered my love for exploring the outdoors.

S. Renay Sanders: Cleveland, Ohio, was the place of my Appalachian home and upbringing. It was there in an enclave of transplants from Tennessee, Kentucky, and West Virginia I learned what it meant to be family, to be loyal, to be other, yet proud. Down home in Grundy County, Tennessee, I experienced traditional music, practical jokes, and storytelling. The music and stories told of living off the land or going north for work. Both were about taking care of your family. In me, those musicians and storytellers morphed into an Appalachian urban poet telling her stories with rhyme, rhythm, and a sense of fun.

Rikki Santer: I was born and raised in the northeastern Ohio area and then spent many fond years living in southeastern Ohio. I think the fact that our state bird is typically the first one to visit feeders in the morning and the last to visit in the evenings is an apt metaphor for the resilience of our people.

Susan Truxell Sauter: I was raised with great trauma in Ohio during my early years. I now regard West Virginia as my home. Conflicted, I periodically haunt back roads to visit that land my forefathers farmed, upon which I also endured. Ohio is where my people are buried and where I visit my developmentally disabled half-brother in a nursing home. While I fiercely identify as Appalachian, it's with deeply conflicted love that I stay.

Karen Schubert: Ohio runs through my blood. I was born in Portsmouth, where my dad was an auditor of the Standard Oil Company of Ohio. My dad's parents lived in Cleveland, my mom's near the Trumbull County fairgrounds where my family has had a claim since the early 1800s. My family moved out of state when I was seven but each summer we met my grandparents at Lakeside, and I operated a ride at Cedar Point the summer of my college freshman year. I moved to Youngstown as an adult, twenty years ago, and own a 1930s house on the Northside.

Roberta Schultz: My dad's grandpa and grandma on his mom's side were from Meigs County before they both moved downriver to the Greater Cincinnati area. My mother's family hailed from Estill County in Kentucky. When my niece got married, it was to a young man from Perry County. They now make their home in the northern tip of Appalachian Ohio, in Somerset. My grandniece is growing up curious about the land as she explores landmarks like Hocking Hills and learns about the wonders of nature.

Sara Shearer: I grew up in the Portage Lakes area just south of Akron, in a town called New Franklin but that the locals call Manchester. If my family members were not born in Akron, they came here from other parts of Appalachia for jobs in the rubber industry. Many of my poems focus on Akron and Manchester, particularly the history of the Nimisila Reservoir. I now live in Cuyahoga Falls.

Susan Sheppard: was a native West Virginian, of Lenni-Lenape (Delaware), Shawnee and European ancestry and descended from some of West Virginia's earliest settlers. She was much beloved by her daughter Scarlet and her Ohio friends across the river with whom she traveled, workshopped poems and shared her extraordinary spiritual experiences.

Colby Smith: I was born in Beckley, West Virginia, and lived there until the age of nineteen when I went to Ohio University in Athens to pursue a BA in geology and minors in paleontology and English. I dropped out to focus on performing punk rock music, writing and work. Now based in Cleveland, I get homesick whenever I hear Appalachian English being spoken, and I am regularly haunted by the ghost of Breece D'J Pancake.

Larry Smith: My people were Appalachian, and I was born and raised in the industrial Ohio River Valley. I am a graduate of Mingo High School, Muskingum University, and Kent State University.

Rose Smith: Now and then, when I read poetry in public, someone will ask, "Where are you from?" and mention "my accent." Traces of Alabama still peek out from me now, decades later. I was raised by grandparents who migrated to Ohio long before I was born, was shuttled back and forth between them and other grandparents still in the South. The imprint will never leave. The rich legacy of a family whose lives were lived on rich red earth and beneath, in its mines, will ever be a part of me even though I breathe Ohio air each day.

Anna Egan Smucker: I was born along the Ohio River in Steubenville, Ohio. We first lived with my mother's family in Toronto, Ohio. Lucky for me, the town's library was right across the street. My aunt checked out armloads of books that she read to me, my favorites over and over. That's what turned me into a reader . . . and a writer. Then we moved to Steubenville where all of our Egan relatives lived. When I was in 3rd Grade, we moved across the river to Weirton, West Virginia. Now, whenever I am anywhere along the beautiful Ohio, I feel like I'm back home.

Sherry Cook Stanforth: A native and resident of Clermont County, I grew up near the Ohio River. I currently live within its sight, near a little town called New Richmond. Every morning, the river cloud rises up through the valley, and I hear the Route 8 train passing along the far shore. I love this place, even as my writing and music reflects storytelling traditions and migration experiences of my Appalachian roots, which stretch toward East Tennessee's Cherohala Skyway and on to North Georgia's Blue Ridge Mountains.

Margo Taft Stever: I grew up in Cincinnati, Ohio, and I lived there until leaving for college. My mother, father, aunts, uncles, grandparents, and great grandparents all came from Cincinnati. Beulah Reid, the nanny who lived with us, and Osborne, a man who also worked at our house, were from Appalachia. We lived as intimately with Appalachians as we did with our own parents. The Appalachian voice became a part of the six children in my family.

Myrna Stone: I was born and raised in the Ohio Valley and have lived here for seventy-four of my seventy-seven years. Though I have lived in small towns, it is the rural landscape that often attracts me.

Colette Tennant: I have deep roots in Ohio's Appalachia. My mother and her mother were born and grew up in Fly, Ohio, a small town on the Ohio River across from Sistersville, West Virginia. It has one of the ferries still in operation. My father was born in Ironton, Ohio and grew up there and in Kentucky. I was born in Columbus, but spent much of my childhood in Fly, staying with my cousins for most summers. My grandparents are buried in Grandview Cemetery on a pretty little hilltop in New Matamoras, Ohio.

Patricia Thrushart: I live over the state's eastern border in the foothills of the Allegheny Mountains, the culture of Northern Appalachia binds us together. As a member of The

Watershed Journal Literary Group and the Writers Association of Northern Appalachia, I have a kinship with Ohio writers immersed in their sense of place. Ohio's role in the Underground Railroad cannot be overstated, and its importance in the abolitionist and anti-slavery activities during the mid-1800s was pivotal.

Kerry Trautman: I was born and raised in Ohio, moving from small town to larger town, back to small town. My poet-ness is virtually inseparable from my Ohio-ness. I count many Appalachians among my friends.

Elizabeth Tussey: I was born in Salem, Ohio, in 1985 and resided there for most of my life. I am a 7th generation Ohio Appalachian. Preceding generations of my family worked in the coalfields and in steel mills along the Ohio River. A number of these ancestors lost their lives in the mines. This ill fortune drove my family to seek answers through superstition and ghost stories. I was raised on these tales—some tall and some truthful. This tradition of storytelling is a deep part of my identity and I feel compelled to preserve and retell stories of Ohio in my writing.

Susan O'Dell Underwood: My connection to Ohio is still awfully tender to me, even after nearly four decades. When I graduated from college in East Tennessee, where I'd always lived, I moved to Columbus, the hometown of my then boyfriend, Dave. We'd been in college together, and he'd moved back to Ohio after graduation. Those early days were traumatic for me because I had not understood what it meant to be "other" or "hillbilly" or Appalachian. I honestly hadn't had an urban experience, much less a "northern" experience. We eventually returned to Tennessee, where we're now an old married couple.

Anastasia Vassos: I was born in Lakewood, Ohio, and grew up on the west side of Cleveland. I spent my first 18 years as a citizen of that city on the shores of Lake Erie. My memories of Appalachia include visiting my father's World War II friend in Weirton, West Virginia, in my early adulthood, visiting friends there: I spent time living and working in the Great Smoky Mountains in Gatlinburg, Tennessee; and I spent a summer with a writer friend on his land in the hills of Brooks, West Virginia.

Randi Ward: After my parents divorced, I spent much of my early teens kicking around Marietta. My father's family hails from Washington County, Ohio. Whenever we visited the homestead, my great-aunt told me stories about a cave where people went to hide from the cruelty of the world. Some of these people, she said, were afflicted with such grief that they were never able to leave the cave; they cried so long and hard that their tears turned to stone, and they faded into darkness. My great-aunt had a bucket full of shiny, black rocks—the tears she'd collected—in her house. I was expected to pick one out of the bucket each visit and take it home with me.

Laura Grace Weldon: I am a lifelong Ohioan. I live on a small homestead in a rural community. My father's people come from Belmont County, where dozens of relatives with the surname Piper still thrive.

Richard Westheimer: In the company of my wife, Debbie, I have lived, gardened, and raised five children on our plot of land in rural Clermont County, Ohio, where we've lived for 45 years. Many of the poems I write are inspired by this plot of land, my longtime friendships with neighbors, our partnership with a family of hunters whose kin hunted there before my time, and by the sounds and weekly experience of picking bluegrass music at the farm down the lane.

Abby Wheeler: I grew up in the village of New Richmond, Ohio, a stone's throw from the river. While I have lived in Cincinnati for the past decade, New Richmond was "home" until my parents moved away just a few short years ago. There are fewer reasons to return these days, but my roots remain there.

Sherrell Wigal: I am an Appalachian by birth and have lived in Appalachia my entire life. In the late 1960s I moved from West Virginia to Ohio and spent several years as an Ohio resident. As a child, several of my Father's siblings moved from West Virginia to Ohio to gain employment, and I spent several weeks each summer visiting them. For over 30 years now, I have resided in Wood County, West Virginia, along the Ohio River. Much of my poetry reflects my love of the Appalachian region and my connection to its people, land, and heritage.

Keith Wilde: I grew up in the village of Norwich, Ohio, population 112, in Muskingum County and for the past 14 years I have lived in Athens, Ohio. These are places where all things are personal, and a life is made by hand. This is not always easy, but others have shown me how to bravely cobble together a living. I feel lucky to reside in these wooded hills among people of insight and ingenuity.

Kristine Williams: I have lived in and written about Athens, Ohio, since 1985, when I came to pursue a master's degree at Ohio University and where I discovered my "place." Years ago, my mother traveled to Pomeroy, Ohio, to do rubbings of headstones of the Geogleins, relations of my paternal grandmother, a connection to this area I didn't know of until then. I continue to be inspired by the hills, hollows, and culture of Appalachia and continue to try to express all that is southeast Ohio in my writing.

Christine Wilson: My Pap-paw unionized the Black Star Mining Co. in Harland County, fighting for safety and pay versus scrip. He was an electrician in the mines, a problem solver, prankster, and a business owner fixing radios, TVs and anything you brought him. Mam-maw cooked, gardened, canned, created ornate quilts, and made and sold dresses. Makes me tired just calling them to mind. I live in Northside (Cincinnati) with my husband and five kids, keeping stories and gratitude alive for the justice, creativity, humor, pride, and deep faith (with a little magic) that runs in my bones.

Scott Woods: I am a life-long resident of Columbus whose family runs several generations deep in the hills of Nelsonville, Dexter, and The Plains, Ohio.

Barry Yeoman: I am originally from Springfield Ohio and currently live in London, Ohio. I have spent most of my working life in blue collar jobs in the Springfield, Dayton area. My list of vocations has been numerous, including stints as a janitor, dock worker, packer, painter, forklift operator, shipping and receiving clerk, assistant high school football coach, consumer affairs rep, and steel conduit machinist. I love the Arts, travel, fishing and Ohio State Buckeye football.

Mark Youssef: I grew up in Kentucky and later moved to Cincinnati as a young adult, where I have lived for the past 10 years. I spent many summers camping, hiking canoeing, foraging for mushrooms, and rock climbing in Appalachia in Kentucky, West Virginia, Ohio, and Tennessee. As a medical student I spent several months doing rural medicine rotations in the region. For one year I lived in a house that backed up to the Appalachian Trail.

Acknowledgments:

Aeolian Harp

Anthology of Appalachia Writers, Volume XI

Blackbird (Grayson Books)

Deep Red (Event Horizon)

Essentially Athens Ohio (Independently Published)

Floyd County Moonshine

Glamoury (Independently Published)

Grey Sparrow Journal

Heaven We Haven't Yet Dreamed (Stubborn Mule Press)

Indiana Voice Journal

Light in the River (Dos Madres)

Loss and Foundering (NightBallet Press)

Mingo Town and Memories (Bottom Dog)

Naugatuk River Review

North Dakota Quarterly

Northern Appalachia Review

ONE ART

Pittsburgh Poetry Journal

Poetry Leaves

Rattle

River Styx Magazine

Rosebud

Sheila-Na-Gig Online

The Laurel Review

Wild Sweet Notes, Fifty years of West Virginia Poetry 1950-1999

Women Speak, Volume Seven (Sheila-Na-Gig Editions)

CPSIA information can be obtained
at www.ICGtesting.com
Printed in the USA
BVHW051449040322
630606BV00002B/2

9 798985 524208